W9-AXE-189

WILLIAM MORRIS AT HOME

WILLIAM MORRIS AT HOME

IN ASSOCIATION WITH THE WILLIAM MORRIS SOCIETY

DAVID RODGERS

EBURY PRESS
LONDON

The William Morris Society was founded in 1956 to make the life, work and ideas of Morris and his circle better known to the world of today. The Society organizes regular lectures and events and publishes a Newsletter and a Journal. Membership forms may be obtained by writing to The William Morris Society, Kelmscott House, 26 Upper Mall, Hammersmith, London W6 9TA enclosing a stamped, self-addressed envelope.

For Yvonne and Tom Jones

First paperback edition published 1996

1 3 5 7 9 10 8 6 4 2

Text copyright © 1996 David Rodgers
Special photography copyright © 1996 Ebury Press

David Rodgers has asserted his right to be identified as the author of this work
under the Copyright, Designs and Patents Act, 1988.

All rights reserved. No part of this publication may be reproduced, stored in a retrieval system,
or transmitted in any form or by any means, electronic, mechanical, photocopying, recording
or otherwise, without the prior permission of the copyright owners.

First published in the United Kingdom in 1996 by Ebury Press
Random House, 20 Vauxhall Bridge Road, London, SW1V 2SA

Random House Australia (Pty) Limited
20 Alfred Street, Milsons Point, Sydney, New South Wales 2061, Australia

Random House New Zealand Limited
18 Poland Road, Glenfield, Auckland 10, New Zealand

Random House South Africa (Pty) Limited
PO Box 337, Bergvlei, South Africa

Random House UK Limited Reg. No. 954009

A CIP catalogue record for this book is available from the British Library.

ISBN 0 09 185820 8

Editor: *Emma Callery*
Design: *Alison Shackleton*
Special Photography: *Sandra Lane*
Stylist: *Marie Willey*
Food Stylist and Recipe Writer: *Lyn Rutherford*
Picture Researcher: *Mary-Jane Gibson*
Printed and bound in Great Britain by Butler & Tanner Limited, Frome and London

PICTURE CREDITS
Hereinafter the following shall be abbreviated as: Bridgeman Art Library – BAL; Hammersmith & Fulham Archives & Local History Collection – HFA; National Monuments Records – NMR; National Portrait Gallery – NPG; The Society of Antiquaries – SOA; Trustees of the British Museum – BM; Trustees of the Board of the Victoria & Albert Museum – V&A; William Morris Gallery – WMG; Private Collection – PC; Royal Commission on the Historical Monuments of England – RCHME.

1 HFA; 3 NPG; 6 WMG; 8 NPG; 9 PC; 11 WMG; 12 NPG; 13 *left* Maas Gallery; 13 *right* PC; 14 National Gallery of Ireland; 15 NPG; 16 NPG; 17 PC/Roy Fox; 18 WMG; 19 BAL; 21 WMG; 22 WMG;

24-25 BAL/Stapleton Coll; 29 Tate Gallery; 33 NMR © RCHME; 35 C.W. Band, Physics Photo Unit, Univ. of Oxford; 36 Ashmolean Museum, Oxford; 39 Tate Gallery; 41 V&A; 43 Carlisle Museum & Art Gallery; 45 PC/Roy Fox; 47 Tate Gallery; 48 NPG; 50 PC; 52 SOA; 58 BAL/V&A; 60 NMR © RCHME; 61 BM; 65 NPG; 66 SOA; 69 BM; 70 V&A; 73 V&A; 75 SOA/Nigel Fisher; 78 Delaware Art Museum, Samuel & Mary R. Bancroft Coll; 79 SOA; 83 Sotheby's; 84 Tate Gallery; 89 NPG; 90 Sotheby's; 93 BM; 94 BM; 97 HFA; 99 NPG; 101 HFA; 102/103 PC/Roy Fox; 105 William Morris Society; 107 NPG; 108 HFA; 111 BAL/V&A; 116 PC/Roy Fox; 121 WMG; 123 PC/Roy Fox; 124 HFA; 126 Cheltenham Art Gallery & Museums: 128 PC/Roy Fox; 129 SOA; 133 BM
All other pictures are by Sandra Lane.

❦ CONTENTS ❦

Foreword   6

Prologue   8

From Elm House to Red House   18

The Red House   40

Queen Square   60

Kelmscott Manor   74

Kelmscott House   96

William Morris and Food   130

Further Reading   158

Index   159

above A STUDIO PORTRAIT OF WILLIAM MORRIS TAKEN AT OXFORD IN 1857

FOREWORD

William Morris was one of the outstanding figures of the nineteenth century; designer, craftsman, social reformer, and visionary. To most people he is an admirable but shadowy Victorian figure, summed up in Max Beebohm's languid dismissal, "Of course he was a wonderful all-round man, but the act of walking round him has always tired me." This book not only offers a lively stroll around Morris, but the prospect of a good meal afterwards if you try the recipes it provides. It is an excellent introduction to this fascinating and complex man, the people he knew and the places where he lived.

Morris is a very attractive character; the more one finds out about him, the more interesting he becomes and this book will, I hope, encourage readers to enquire further into his life, work and ideas. He was devoted to his family, created a famous design company, pursued an astonishing variety of arts – drawing, painting, embroidery, weaving, dyeing, block printing, stained glass, calligraphy, woodcuts, and type and book design. His thought, imagination and practical skills were prodigious, but he remained unpretentious and anything but pompous. Passionate about the countryside, architecture, literature, education, art and equality, he delivered his opinions with characteristic vigour.

In his lifetime he was best known as a poet, the author of *The Earthly Paradise*. Today, his fame rests chiefly on his designs for wallpapers and fabrics which changed the decor of Victorian interiors. Few realize that he was also a visionary political and social theorist who ruined his health speaking at street corners and meeting halls throughout the country. His ideas, for instance on how we might live more satisfactory lives in which, as for him, art would play a central role, are as relevant today as they were to his contemporaries.

The William Morris Society brings together all those interested in Morris in every part of the world. He has been influential in America, Japan, Australia and all over Europe – and given the range of his interests that makes for a diverse and varied group with a Journal, a Newsletter, and an active programme of lectures, study weekends, and visits inspired, we hope, by his own words, "Fellowship is Life".

The Society is pleased to be associated with our Curator, David Rodgers, and Ebury Press in the publication of this book. Needless to say, the opinions expressed are the author's alone, but he shows Morris as the approachable figure he is: talented, many-sided, an example of humanity and courage to us all. I am delighted to be able to recommend this first course – what a splendid meal awaits the reader.

HANS BRILL FSA
PRESIDENT, WILLIAM MORRIS SOCIETY

PROLOGUE

"Comrade Morris is not dead, there is not a Socialist living would believe him dead for he lives in the heart of all true men and women still and will do so to the end of time."

RESOLUTION OF THE LANCASHIRE BRANCH OF THE
SOCIAL DEMOCRATIC FEDERATION (OCTOBER 1896)

WILLIAM MORRIS DIED ON THE MORNING of Saturday 3 October 1896 in his bedroom at his London home, Kelmscott House, Hammersmith. He was 62 years old. Inside the room were his wife Jane, May, his younger daughter, his friends Georgiana Burne-Jones and Mary de Morgan and a recent disciple, Detmar Blow. Blow, a young architect, was a friend of Morris's secretary and librarian Sidney Cockerell and it was almost certainly the latter – ambitious, ingratiating but coolly efficient – who organized Morris's funeral and had already prepared for his burial, knowing that his employer was dying.

By the afternoon, Morris's corpse lay in an elm-wood shell, lined with swansdown, which had been delivered by the undertakers, Barratts of Chiswick. They returned on the Sunday morning with a smooth, unpolished oak coffin "of special design", with wrought iron handles and an inscription, designed by Blow, carved on the lid. The funeral took place the following Tuesday. Outside the riverside house, the Thames ran grey beneath a threatening overcast sky as the coffin was placed in a glass-sided hearse drawn by two brown horses. Followed by two closed Broughams, they bore the dead poet to Paddington Station, the London terminus of the Great Western Railway Company. Morris was taking his last journey from his detested London to his beloved Kelmscott, the Oxfordshire hamlet which had been his country retreat since 1871.

Joined by family and friends, the funeral party travelled to Oxford from Paddington and then to the small market town of Lechlade by special train. They reached Lechlade in the late morning and in heavy rain which was to worsen dramatically as the day wore on, flooding the low-lying fields around the Upper Thames.

Here formality gave way to rusticity. The formal, black, crepe-wreathed top hats and frockcoats of the London undertakers (one of whom had accompanied the mourners), were replaced by the picturesque garments of four moleskin-clad farm-workers. They bore the coffin to a gaily decorated Hay-waggon, yellow of body and red of wheel, which had been entwined with vines and strewn with willow boughs, and placed the coffin upon a carpet of moss. The coffin was then draped with a favourite piece from Morris's extensive collection of rare fabrics, a fine antique piece of Broussa brocade, rich silk from Turkey, on which was placed a wreath of bay.

The creator and driver of this strange Arcadian hearse was Detmar Blow, appropriately dressed in a wide-sleeved haymaker's smock. He set off at a stately pace through the dripping country lanes to Kelmscott, followed by the mourners in eleven carriages. These were decidedly more practical and had been hired by Cockerell from the New Inn at Lechlade.

The service was held in the small twelfth-century village church that had been repaired, but not restored, with the help of generous donations

previous page left A STUDIO PORTRAIT OF WILLIAM MORRIS TAKEN IN THE 1890S.

previous page right THE RUSTIC FUNERAL CART WHICH BORE WILLIAM MORRIS'S COFFIN FROM LECHLADE STATION TO KELMSCOTT CHURCH.

from Morris. It was conducted by the Rev. WF Adams, vicar of the nearby parish of Little Faringdon, a contemporary of Morris at both Marlborough and Oxford. The address was brief and the church *en fete*, festooned with fruit, vegetables and flowers for the Harvest Festival.

The congregation numbered about forty and was strangely incongruous, representing as it did all the stages of Morris's life and all facets of his career. They were united only by their love of Morris. Jane and May Morris had been joined at Kelmscott Manor by his elder daughter Jenny, and Elizabeth "Bessie" Burden, Jane's sister. May's estranged husband Halliday Sparling, the erstwhile and ineffectual Secretary of the Kelmscott Press, also attended, having returned poste haste from Paris. Two of Morris's four sisters, Henrietta, a Catholic convert, and Isabella Gilmore, who had become an Anglican Deaconess after her husband's early death, were present, as were two of his three surviving brothers. These were Edgar, the youngest brother and previously employed by Morris, and either Stanley, a gentleman farmer, or Colonel Arthur Morris, a retired career soldier.

As for the rest, there were present Ned and Georgie Jones, now, to the latter's annoyance, Sir Edward and Lady Burne-Jones; Cormell Price and the Pre-Raphaelite painter Arthur Hughes, early friends from Oxford days; Morris's publisher and fellow angler, FS Ellis, who knew Kelmscott well having shared the lease of the Manor with Morris between 1874 and 1884; and socialist comrades who included the autocratic and wealthy HM Hyndman, the working class John Burns, now an MP, and the romantic, flame-haired Robert Cunninghame Graham who thought Jane Morris, on this occasion, to be six feet tall and, swathed in her widow's weeds, almost as wide.

Bridging the gap between art and politics were Emery Walker, Morris's Hammersmith neighbour and adviser on the Kelmscott Press, who had cared for him selflessly and tirelessly during his final illness, and the painter and designer Walter Crane, both of them members of the Hammersmith Socialist Society. Later admirers, from the world of Arts and Crafts, included Blow, the architect and designer WR Lethaby and

above JANE MORRIS AND ONE OF HER DAUGHTERS IN THE 1860S.

the fastidious Cockerell. Kelmscott villagers, workmen from the Morris Factory at Merton Abbey, and salesmen from the Morris shop in Oxford Street made up the congregation.

The storm ceased briefly as Morris was interred, to lie in his beloved Kelmscott earth under a tombstone. A simple raised slab of shallow triangular section, it was based on a traditional local type, and designed by his great and faithful friend Philip Webb.

After the service, family and friends returned to the old grey Manor House along the sodden village street and forty of them sat down to a funeral lunch which had been delivered from the Swan Inn at Lechlade at a cost of half a crown a head. Some of the complexities of Morris's life may be seen reflected in his funeral. The diversity of the congregation reveals his many interests, and the unconventionality of his position in Victorian society is symbolized by the bizarre progress of his corpse from House to Manor. *The Bard and Petty Tradesman*, caricatured by Dante

left JOHN RUSKIN AND DANTE GABRIEL ROSSETTI IN 1863.

above left EDWARD BURNE-JONES IN 1864, AGED 31.

above right GEORGIANA MACDONALD, LATER BURNE-JONES, IN 1857, AGED 16.

far left JANE BURDEN, AGED 18, DRAWN BY DG ROSSETTI DURING A BRIEF VISIT TO OXFORD WHEN MORRIS WAS ABSENT IN FRANCE.

left PHILIP WEBB, PAINTED BY CHARLES FAIRFAX MURRAY IN 1873.

Gabriel Rossetti in 1866, left his London home with all the pompous trappings of the *Petty Tradesman* and arrived at his grave with the laurel leaves of the *Bard*.

The "simple coffin", referred to by most of his biographers, may indeed have been simple but it was by no means ordinary or inexpensive, a paradox which Morris had been deeply conscious of throughout his career as a manufacturer. And for the final irony, and despite the Bacchic trappings of his hearse, Morris – the self-confessed unbeliever and pagan – received a conventional Christian burial. Victorian respectability, "mumbo-jumbo" as Morris described it, triumphed at the last.

Morris died of tuberculosis, but according to his first biographer JW Mackail, the Burne-Joneses' son-in-law, at least one doctor diagnosed the cause of death as "being William Morris, and having done more work

above A STUDIO PORTRAIT OF FORD MADOX BROWN TAKEN IN THE EARLY 1870S.

right A TILE IN THE GARDEN PORCH AT RED HOUSE DECORATED WITH MORRIS'S MOTTO, "SI JE PUIS", WHICH HE ADAPTED FROM THAT OF THE FIFTEENTH-CENTURY FLEMISH PAINTER JAN VAN EYCK IN THE LATE 1850S.

than most ten men". Morris's output is phenomenal by any standards. He averred that there was nothing that a man could not learn in half a day, and during the forty years of his adult life and following his own precept taught himself drawing, painting, carving, calligraphy and illumination, block-cutting, dyeing, weaving, tapestry and embroidery.

He created over 600 designs for papers, textiles and embroidery, over 150 for stained glass, and three typefaces and roughly 650 borders and ornaments for the Kelmscott Press. The Press, which he established in 1890, published 52 works in 66 volumes. Believing that a man who couldn't compose an epic poem while weaving a tapestry wasn't much of a man, Morris wrote over thirty books of verse, fiction, translation and political theory, one of which, alone, *The Earthly Paradise*, published between 1868 and 1870, contains 42,000 lines of rhyming verse.

This was not all. From the mid-1870s, he was a successful business man, manufacturer and retailer and, after 1877, a very active political theorist and agitator for Socialism. He wrote over 100 lectures and speeches and, despite his innate shyness, delivered them throughout the country. On Sunday mornings, although troubled by both rheumatism and gout, he could usually be found on a soap-box, beside Hammersmith bridge, competing with the Salvationists for the attention of reluctant passers-by.

Morris's motto was adapted from that of the fifteenth-century Flemish painter, Jan van Eyck. It was "If I can", in his case meaning, if I can I will, and he lived up to it magnificently.

This book, while not ignoring his achievements and disappointments in art and politics, concentrates on Morris's domestic activities, his leisure interests (for, amazingly, he found time to relax), and way of life. More particularly, as the title makes clear, it looks at the places where he lived, for places, and homes, were of paramount importance to Morris. "The house and the household", wrote Mackail, "with all that these words involve, were, to Morris, the symbol and the embodiment of civilised human life."

As Morris himself wrote in 1884, "It is not an original remark, but I make it here, that my home is where I meet people with whom I sympathise, whom I love."

From Elm House to Red House

"He has tinged my whole inner being with the beauty of his own"

EDWARD BURNE-JONES (1854)

WILLIAM MORRIS WAS BORN ON 24 March 1834, at Elm House, Clay Hill, Walthamstow, Essex. His parents William and Elizabeth (née Shelton), already had two daughters and a son, Charles, who had died in infancy in 1837, and the young William was to have a further two sisters and four brothers. His father, whose family were of Welsh origin, was a successful city financier and Elm House, although by no means grand, was a substantial square residence in what was then a village, beyond the north eastern suburbs of London.

Morris was a much cossetted child, brought up as a semi-invalid by his over-protective parents, made anxious by the loss of their first son. His eldest sister, Emma, for whom Morris retained a lasting devotion, had been born in 1829 and so was old enough to take a keen interest in her baby brother and let him play with her precious dolls and miniature tea set. The children would certainly have had a nurse and would doubt-less have seen little of their ambitious father during the working week.

By 1840, the family were sufficiently prosperous to take a lease, at £600 a year, on Woodford Hall, an imposing Italianate mansion on the fringe of Epping Forest. Woodford Hall was a house fit for a gentleman and in 1843 William Morris, senior, became one by successfully applying for a coat of arms. This apparently trivial act was not without significance in mid-nineteenth century England. It was an age of great social change as fortunes were made and lost, families moved from country to town, and the rigid class structure of the previous century was in disarray. It was important for the rapidly expanding middle classes to know their place in society and the newly armigerous Morrises had now established themselves as gentry.

Woodford Hall was the first of William Morris's three Edens and his childhood experiences there coloured the rest of his life. By his own account it was idyllic. The estate was largely self-supporting with farm, bakery, dairy and brewery, well-stocked orchards and kitchen gardens. Morris's greed in later years suggests that he haunted the kitchen, spoilt by cook and maid. Like all the children, he was given his own small gar-den which ignited a lifelong interest in botany and horticulture, and he loved to play or simply lie among the fruit trees which, again, became a recurrent motif in adulthood.

Morris claimed never to have consciously been taught to read but to have read all Scott's novels before he was seven. His own opinion, as a parent, was that children taught each other, and, as a child, he probably benefitted from Emma's informal tuition. Scott remained a favourite writer, and his novels were the inspiration for Morris's solitary games in Epping forest. On foot or pony, sometimes wearing a miniature suit of armour, he roamed the rides and glades, dreaming of knights in armour, mortal combats and virginal damsels.

previous page left ELM HOUSE, WALTHAMSTOW, THE SOLID NINETEENTH-CENTURY VILLA IN WHICH MORRIS WAS BORN IN 1834.

previous page right A SELF-CARICATURE OF JONES EXAMINING A "MEDIAEVAL" CHAIR AT RED LION SQUARE. THE BROKEN CHAIRS AND CRUMPLED CLOTHES BEHIND HIM ARE EVIDENCE OF MORRIS'S OCCUPANCY.

WOODFORD HALL. ESSEX.

In this same forest, playing among the hornbeams, he discovered his passionate and undying love of nature, the magnificence of trees and the individuality of landscape. In 1895, a year before he died, he wrote to the *Daily Chronicle*, fearful of threats to his beloved Epping Forest, "When I was a boy and young man (I) knew it yard by yard from Wanstead to the Theydons, and from Hale End to the Fairlop Oak." This he undoubtedly did, for his powers of observation were abnormally acute. Morris's attitude to nature is almost mystic, almost sexual; he embraced it, loved it and, so far as he could, protected it.

It was in Epping Forest, too, that he discovered his great love of architecture, and his instinctive response to it. "How well I remember", he wrote in 1882, "as a boy my first acquaintance with a room hung with faded greenery at Queen Elizabeth's Lodge, by Chingford Hatch, in Epping Forest... and the impression of romance that it made upon me." He is writing, of course, of his reaction to an individual room, but the Lodge itself had a profound effect on him. The building had evolved from a sixteenth-century pavilion, built for Henry VIII to observe the hunt when he had grown too obese and gouty to take part. To the young

above WOODFORD HALL, ESSEX, THE FAMILY HOME FROM 1840 UNTIL MORRIS'S FATHER'S DEATH IN 1847.

romantic Morris, steeped in Scott, it must have seemed deeply mysterious, isolated in the woods, partly ramshackle, almost organic, a building that had changed and aged as the trees that surrounded it had changed and aged.

In 1847, Morris's father died at the early age of fifty. Morris seldom, if ever, spoke of his father but he seems to have taken the unexpected death stoically. He seems to have been equally robust about two other major changes in his life: being sent away to Marlborough College, Wiltshire, and leaving Woodford Hall for a smaller house at Walthamstow.

The move to Marlborough College had been planned before his father died and Morris had been boarding weekly at a local school to acclimatize him for leaving home. The fees posed no problem as Morris, senior, had made a particularly lucrative investment in a copper mine not long before he died. Although the family were undoubtedly worse off, they were still, in Morris's blunt words of the 1880s, "rich in fact." The income from the dividends and occasional sales of Devon Great Consols made Morris's subsequent life possible.

Marlborough had been founded only six years before Morris arrived in 1847 and drew most of its pupils from the sons of Anglican clergy. Despite their vicarage backgrounds, the majority of the boys were unruly and bullying was common. Morris soon learnt to survive by fighting when necessary and disarming when possible, by humour and the telling of tales. His nickname was Crab, quite possibly because of his hobby of making fishing nets, but with typical schoolboy accuracy the name suggests an armoured awkwardness, and a solitary perseverance which, from what we know of Morris's schooldays, is remarkably apt.

Morris claimed to have learnt nothing at Marlborough, but it would be more strictly true to say that he was taught nothing for he learnt a great deal by establishing a pattern of self-education which he continued into adulthood. The college library was well stocked and he read avidly and widely. In his free time, presumably at weekends, he explored the surrounding countryside, visiting the local churches and glorying in the prehistoric monuments of Avebury and Silbury Hill.

above WATER HOUSE, WALTHAMSTOW. EMMA MORRIS MOVED HERE WITH HER FAMILY IN 1848 IN ORDER TO ECONOMIZE, AND STAYED UNTIL 1856.

His holidays were spent at Water House in Walthamstow, with his family. The house, which now houses the William Morris Gallery, was a handsome mid-eighteenth-century building with a double-bow front and, although it lacked the splendid woods and parkland of Woodford Hall, it had spacious gardens which included a wide moat, suitable for rowing and fishing.

Morris was withdrawn from Marlborough in December 1851, shortly after a serious riot at the school which had alarmed many parents and resulted in the resignation of the sadly incompetent Head. Morris, willingly or not, was intended for the Church as befitted a gentleman's son, and it was therefore essential that he should go on to University. So, in order to achieve Oxford entry he was enroled for tuition with a local schoolmaster, the Rev. Frederick Guy, a High Anglican from whom he learnt Latin, Greek and theology, and also the principles of self-denial and service to others which the Anglo-Catholic movement stressed. As a young man already steeped in fictional chivalry, Morris was particularly receptive to these high ideals.

He sat his Oxford matriculation examination in June 1852, and entered Exeter College, which had close links with Marlborough, in 1853. Oxford, largely unchanged since the fifteenth century, appeared magical to Morris. On his schoolboy expeditions, he had of course seen medieval buildings, but never a medieval townscape, nor the particular combination of religious and secular architecture to be found in the ancient colleges, redolent of brotherhood, scholarship and devotion. It remained one of the great loves of his life, and its despoliation in later years caused him both anger and anguish. Exeter, however, he found less to his taste. The college was dominated by "Hearties", fast-living and hard-drinking men with whom he had little in common. Fortunately, among the new intake of undergraduates, Morris found a soul-mate who was to remain his closest friend for the rest of his life.

Edward Jones, a year older than Morris, came from a very different background. He had been brought up in Birmingham by his widower father, a frame-maker by trade, in polite poverty, and through his own efforts, rather than parental money, had gained a place at King Edward's School. He was a slim, virtually frail, boy, imaginative and excitable and, by the time he arrived in Oxford, his hair was beginning to thin. The two men met on their first day at Exeter and found themselves immediately compatible. Both were intelligent, both were high-minded, both were destined for the priesthood and, above all, both were in love with an imaginary medieval past.

Jones introduced Morris to his school friends, William Fulford and Richard Watson Dixon, both Pembroke men, who, together with Charles Faulkner and Cormell Price (who came up a year later), provided him

"It was a fortunate circumstance that he was never cramped by poverty in the development of his aims."

WALTER CRANE, 1911

with an instant circle of sympathetic and loyal friends. The Set, as they called themselves, was the first and most lasting of the close groups of male friends which were so important to Morris.

It was Dixon, years later, who described Morris as an "aristocrat". Initially, he must indeed have been a somewhat incongruous member of The Set, for his wealth and social standing was noticeably different from their own. It was possibly as an attempt to hide this, to reduce himself to their equal, that Morris adopted the role of buffoon which he was not to abandon until his thirties; teasing Morris became the common pursuit of his friends, which was not without its dangers. This doubtless added to their enjoyment, for Morris would fly into the most alarming tempers, quite literally "fits" of temper, which Fiona MacCarthy, his most recent biographer, has convincingly suggested were epileptic in origin. He was normally the most peaceful of men and, when annoyed, capable of prodigious self-control, but these occasional explosions, frightening to those who witnessed them, continued until his death.

Perhaps it was for the same reason – to deny his Father's hard-earned gentility – that by the time he left Oxford, Morris had taken to swearing. "Damme" appears to have been his most common expletive but used so frequently and with such force as to be critically noticed by his friends. He could not, however, entirely escape from the legacy of his class and background. He was often thoughtless and arrogant and, although never a snob, his occasional high-handedness was particularly observed and resented by his social inferiors. These traits, together with other aspects of his personality, were known by his friends as "Topsaic" or "Topsian".

In appearance, Morris was stocky, and later, stout, with a mass of curly black hair which earned him the nickname "Topsy", for, like the little black girl in *Uncle Tom's Cabin* it "grow'd". At Oxford he was clean shaven but on leaving he sported a moustache and an exiguous beard, which grew bushy in middle age. His eyes were blue and his gaze was unresponsive, which was disconcerting to some contemporaries. He seems to have already become a "fidgett", which both he and others commented upon, unable to keep still for any length of time, and had an unfortunate habit of clenching the muscles in his broad back which, when seated, demolished all but the strongest of chairs.

According to Crom Price, writing in 1857, Morris was also untidy: "Rossetti said that Topsy had the greatest capacity for producing and annexing dirt of any man he ever met with." And he was forgetful, another source of merriment to his friends and, mixed with annoyance, to Morris himself who was well aware of this failing. In later life, his daughter tells us, he would inscribe the fly-leaf of his notebook, "If you find this book bring it to the owner, W. Morris, 26 Queen Square, Bloomsbury, and you shall be rewarded."

Physically he was very strong. Although he avoided most sports, he excelled at single-stick, perhaps because of its medieval associations. According to Archibald Maclaren, the owner of the Gymnasium and Fencing Club in Oriel Lane which Morris patronized, he was renowned for the number of hefty sticks he broke.

Jones and Morris were Anglo-Catholics, followers of the Tractarian Movement, founded by John Henry Newman in the 1840s, which proclaimed Catholicism to be the true religion and the Church of England to be the true Catholic church. Newman had seceded to the Roman Church in 1845 and was soon followed by other luminaries, Henry Wilberforce, in 1850, and Henry Manning in 1851. In Oxford, the flame of Anglo-Catholicism was kept flickering by Professor Pusey, whose sermons they both admired. But the Church of Morris and Jones was on the wane and, in 1854, when Robert Wilberforce joined his brother Henry in the Roman Catholic Church, "he all but carried them with him".

Jones, who parodied his love of ritual and ancient rites by signing letters to his friends, "Edouard, Cardinal de Birminghame", was more deeply distressed than the pragmatic Morris and it was probably he who first resolved upon the idea of a "Brotherhood" which pre-occupied the friends between 1853 and 1855.

According to Lady Burne-Jones, writing many years later, the Brotherhood would have been "a small conventual society of cleric and lay members working in the heart of London". But this is certainly a rationalization, the Brotherhood recollected in tranquillity. To Morris and Jones, the concept of Brotherhood owed as much to chivalry as to theology. "Remember", wrote Jones to Cormell Price in May 1853, "I have set my heart on our founding a Brotherhood... Learn Sir Galahad by heart. He is to be the Patron of our Order."

The appeal of the Brotherhood, which was to be financed by Morris, was essentially escapist. It offered the friends theological resolution by withdrawal from the current schismatic controversies; emotional sanctuary, by espousing chastity, and, most importantly, a way of stopping the world, a retreat, in the literal sense of the word, from society.

Their aversion to the times they lived in was, in part, the result of their reading, and it was not peculiar to them. The Middle Ages offered more than romance to the Victorians, it seemed to them to be a time when society was stable and transactions between man and his fellows were honourable and disinterested; it offered idealism in an age of compromise and beauty in an age of "shoddy". All The Set were Tennysonians, and particularly well-versed in the *Morte d'Arthur*, based on the Arthurian legend, which had been published in 1842.

The emotional appeal of fiction was reinforced by the social critiques of Thomas Carlyle and John Ruskin. The former's *Past and Present* (1843),

"We must enlist you, dear Brother, in this crusade and Holy Warfare against the age, 'the heartless coldness of the times'."

EDWARD JONES
IN A LETTER TO CORMELL PRICE

previous page OXFORD IN 1793. IT HAD HARDLY CHANGED WHEN MORRIS WENT UP IN 1853.

was a sustained attack on nineteenth-century industrialized capitalism, comparing it unfavourably with an idealized picture of life in the twelfth-century monastery of St Edmundsbury. Carlyle's exhortation, "Behold, supply and demand is not the one law of Nature; cash payment is not the sole nexus of man with man – how far from it! Deep, far deeper than supply and demand are laws, obligations sacred as man's life itself", must have been one of the earliest seeds of Morris's later socialism.

The book that had the most profound effect on Morris, changed the course of his life, and formed the basis of much of his future philosophy, was the second volume of John Ruskin's *Stones of Venice*, published in 1853 during his first year at Oxford. Although only in his thirties, Ruskin had already established himself as a formidable critic of art and architecture and his writings were greatly admired by Morris. The first volume of *Stones of Venice*, had been published in 1851 and Morris rushed out to buy volume two as soon as it appeared. He had doubtless read *The Seven Lamps of Architecture* of 1849, which established the architectural hierarchy he adhered to for the rest of his life. Put at its simplest, for Ruskin and his young disciple, Gothic architecture was good and Classical architecture was bad.

The Stones of Venice went further, for a chapter in the second volume, "The Nature of Gothic", for the first time equated the beauties of medieval architecture and ornament with the pleasure that was taken by the workmen in executing them. From this proposition, Ruskin went on to argue that the architecture of a society is the outward reflection of its moral worth. To Morris this came as a complete revelation. Years later, in 1892, in the preface to the Kelmscott Press edition of *The Nature of Gothic*, he wrote that it was "one of the very few necessary and inevitable utterances of the century."

In October 1854, at the beginning of their final year, Morris and Jones had adjoining rooms in the Old Buildings of Exeter College. Morris's rooms were "pleasant ones overlooking Exeter Garden and the Schools, in a little quadrangle that was called Hell Quad. You passed under an archway called Purgatory from the Great Quadrangle to reach it." The two were virtually inseparable and Jones, self-confessedly, in a letter to Price, hero-worshipped Morris. "He has tinged my whole inner being with the beauty of his own, and I know not a single gift for which I owe such gratitude to Heaven as his friendship". Only his "Topsaic" behaviour marred his perfection, for Jones continued, "If it were not for his boisterous mad outbursts and freaks, which break the romance he sheds around him – at least to me – he would be a perfect hero."

Morris and Jones still frequented Pembroke and The Set. Early in 1855 Morris wrote his first poem, "The Willow and the Cliff", and from now on he was often called upon to recite his own verse, "Give us one of your

grinds, Morris", to the group of friends. "Well, if this is poetry", said Morris, "it is very easy to write."

At the end of the summer term, Morris, Jones and Fulford set off for an expedition in northern France. Morris had been there the year before with his elder sister Henrietta during a holiday which also took in Bruges. Bruges remained one of his favourite cities and it was probably here that he first saw the motto "Als ich Kann", "When I can", on the paintings of Jan van Eyck, a motto he adopted to "If I can" and took as his own. Now he wished to share his enthusiasm for French Gothic architecture with his friends and, sympathetic to Jones's poverty, suggested a walking tour.

above THE TUNE OF SEVEN TOWERS BY DANTE GABRIEL ROSSETTI, ONE OF THE SIX WATERCOLOURS PURCHASED BY MORRIS IN 1856 AND 1857.

They started from Folkestone on 19 July taking the ferry to Boulogne and proceeded by train to Abbeville where they stayed the night. Next morning they explored the cathedral where Jones made a number of drawings. Late in the afternoon they reached Amiens where Morris developed a limp and filled the streets "with imprecations on all boot-makers." As his feet were too swollen to be comfortable in leather he purchased a pair of gaily coloured carpet-slippers and hobbled along in his eccentric footwear to Beauvais, a distance of ten miles. Here he declared that the walking part of the tour was over. It is quite possible, given his impatience and his generosity, that his lameness was an elaborate subterfuge to force Jones to accept a subsidy for the remainder of the tour.

Finding themselves in Beauvais on a Sunday they attended High Mass in the cathedral, "The most beautiful church in the world", according to the impressionable Jones. Here the other two prevailed upon a reluctant Morris to continue to Paris where he was mollified by seeing seven English Pre-Raphaelite paintings in the Beaux-Arts Exhibition. One evening was spent at the Opera where, Fulford noted, "Jones was perfectly enraptured, but Morris seemed a good deal bored." After three days in Paris they visited Chartres; Rouen, a city which enchanted him; Caudebec, and Le Havre.

It was here, on the Quay, that the two earnest young friends, fired by the wonders they had seen, decided to abandon all intentions of entering the priesthood and "begin a life of art." Religion, they felt, had failed society, but great art could change it. "The essence of what Ruskin taught us was really nothing more recondite than this, that the art of any epoch must of necessity be the expression of its social life", wrote Morris, years later. It followed that by changing the nature of art they could change the nature of society. Jones would become a painter and Morris an architect. According to Jones, "That was the most memorable night of my Life."

Once back in England, having seen "Nine Cathedrals and 24 splendid churches, some of them surpassing 1st class English Cathedrals", as Morris enthused to Price, he visited Birmingham to stay with Jones. Shortly before his arrival, the latter had discovered a copy of Southey's edition of Malory's *Morte d'Arthur* in a bookshop in New Street. By dint of making daily purchases of the cheapest books, he had managed to read most of it without enraging the shopkeeper. This was a book that was to enthral them both, the source of Tennyson's poem, the *ultima dicta* of chivalry. Morris, when told of his friend's wonderful discovery, bought it and had it bound in white vellum.

Others of The Set were in Birmingham during the Oxford vacation and they met frequently, if irregularly. It was at one of these social gatherings that Dixon suggested that they should publish a monthly journal. Wilfred Heeley, an Old Edwardian up at Cambridge, was also present and thus *The Oxford and Cambridge Magazine* was founded. It would contain original fiction in prose and verse, and critical articles; if funds permitted original illustrations would also be included. However, as Cormell Price recorded, there was to be no "shewing-off, no quips, no sneers, no lampooning", and no politics. The enterprise would be funded by Morris who was now an extremely wealthy young man, having come into an income of £900 a year when he attained his majority in 1855.

The Oxford and Cambridge Magazine lasted for one year and appeared as twelve monthly issues. Morris's contribution, other than financial, included several poems and a number of tales which established his practice, often used in later literary work, of setting his story within a dream. He also published a piece on Amiens cathedral which reveals something of the process whereby he arrived at an appreciation of architecture. "I thought that if I could say nothing else about these grand churches, I could at least tell men how I loved them. For I will say here that I think these same churches of North France the grandest, the most beautiful, the kindest and most loving of all the buildings that the earth has ever borne." Here Morris attributes feelings to architecture, the churches are "kind" and "loving". Later, Philip Webb was to remark that Morris's knowledge of architectural history was instinctive and that he knew ancient buildings as though he had built them. Buildings spoke to Morris and he judged them by the human qualities with which he endowed them.

Jones also contributed to the first issue in January 1856. In an essay on *The Newcomes*, a recently published novel by Thackeray, he contrived to praise the work of the Pre-Raphaelite painter Dante Gabriel Rossetti. Both Morris and Jones had long admired Pre-Raphaelite painting, to which they had been introduced by Ruskin's essay on the movement, written in 1851. Apart from the works they had seen in Paris, they had admired Millais' *Return of the Dove to the Ark* when it was exhibited at Wyatt's gallery in Oxford in 1854, and had made a pilgrimage to Tottenham to see Benjamin Windus's collection in 1855. *The Oxford and Cambridge Magazine* was partly inspired by *The Germ*, the long defunct journal founded by the Pre-Raphaelite Brotherhood. When Jones had taken the decision to become a painter, on the Quay of Le Havre the man he most wanted as his master was Rossetti.

In January 1856, as the first issue of *The Oxford and Cambridge Magazine* appeared in the booksellers, price one shilling, Morris joined the office of the Gothic Revival architect George Edmund Street, in Beaumont Street, Oxford, and signed his articles of pupillage on 21 January. His decision to study under Street, rather than another architect, was considered and deliberate. Morris had met Street at meetings of the Oxford Plainsong Society, and the two men were already friends.

Furthermore, Morris wished to remain in Oxford, a city he loved and where he still had friends.

Morris's day to day supervision at Street's was the responsibility of Philip Webb, his senior by three years. Webb was the son of a country doctor but had spent much of his youth in Oxford and was able to introduce Morris to aspects of the city and its architecture that were new to him. The two became firm and lifelong friends. Webb, who never married, showed a loyalty to Morris which certainly equalled, and in some ways surpassed that of Jones.

In the same momentous January of 1856, when Morris entered Street's office, Jones was meeting his hero. The meeting took place at the Working Men's College where Rossetti, at Ruskin's instigation, had been taking life classes for the last year. Jones turned up in the hope of seeing Rossetti and was overjoyed when a fellow teacher, Vernon Lushington, introduced him to the Master.

Dante Gabriel Rossetti was only five years older than Jones but infinitely more experienced in the ways of the world. He was famous both as a poet, admittedly scarcely published, and as a painter. He had been one of the principal founders of the Pre-Raphaelite Brotherhood and numbered Ruskin and Browning among his friends, and Tennyson among his acquaintances. In short, he was a Prince among Bohemians, exotic and slightly dangerous. His appearance was unprepossessing; he was of average height but balding and growing stout, the latter a result of his extreme physical indolence. But Rossetti's attractiveness did not depend on outward appearances, he was charismatic and his charm was irresistible. He was generous and expansive at this time of his life and immediately welcomed the deliriously happy Jones as his pupil. As a teacher his technical skills were wanting, what he taught was enthusiasm and confidence. Jones had few lessons and those he had were probably inadequate, but for the rest of his life (according to his own testimony), he always asked himself whether Gabriel would have approved.

Jones introduced Morris to Dante Gabriel Rossetti at the first possible opportunity and during his weekend visits from Oxford, Morris too fell under Gabriel's spell. After George Street moved his architect's office to London in June 1856, Morris and Jones shared rooms in Upper Gordon Square but after a few weeks, enchanted by all things Rossettian, they decided to move, at his suggestion, to 17 Red Lion Square where he himself had lived in 1851, with the dying young painter Walter Deverell. Initially, Morris continued to work in Street's office by day and accompany Jones to a drawing class in the evenings but his heart was no longer in architecture and by the autumn of that year, he had abandoned his studies and was determined to become a painter because "Rossetti says I ought to paint."

right NUMBER 17 RED LION SQUARE; MORRIS AND JONES LIVED ON THE FIRST FLOOR FROM NOVEMBER 1856 UNTIL EARLY 1859 IN ROOMS WHICH HAD BEEN OCCUPIED BY ROSSETTI IN 1851.

Shortly before they moved into Rossetti's old rooms Jones had become engaged to Georgiana MacDonald, the fifteen-year-old daughter of a Methodist minister, but Red Lion Square was very much a bachelor establishment. They rented three rooms on the first floor: a large front room, which they used as a studio, and two rear bedrooms of which Morris, typically, had the smaller. The rooms were unfurnished and Morris immediately set about finding furniture. Not that any furniture would do. Morris, probably aided by Webb, designed his own in a style that he considered medieval and had it made by a local carpenter. This furniture was massive, made from planks of unvarnished wood, and some of it, like the solid round dining table now in Cheltenham Art Gallery, may still be seen.

Rossetti was intrigued by this archaic furniture and described it to his friend William Allingham as looking "like incubi and succubi". The chairs, one of which was surmounted by an open box in which he maintained an owl should be kept, particularly interested him and may well have inspired the bizarre thrones that appear in his watercolours of this period. The finest of these, *The Tune of Seven Towers* and *The Blue Closet*, were purchased by Morris and inspired him to poetry. Initially Rossetti probably saw Morris as a patron as much as a painter. He described him to Allingham as "a millionaire" and, indeed, for a brief period Morris was an active collector, buying Arthur Hughes's *April Love* and Madox Brown's *Hayfield* as well as a further five Rossetti watercolours.

The furniture was not left plain but was painted by Morris, Jones and Rossetti with scenes from Malory and Chaucer. The completion of a piece was a cause for celebration, "Come tonight and see the chair", wrote Jones to Madox Brown in 1858, "There's a dear old fellow – such a chair!!!!!! Gabriel and Top hook it tomorrow, so do come, Hughes will come, and a stunner or two to make melody. Come soon, there's a nice old chap -victuals and squalor at all hours, but come at six." One of the "stunners" was his fiancée Georgiana who played the piano hired for the occasion.

In the studio at Red Lion Square, Morris began the first of his only two oil paintings, *How Sir Tristram was recognized by his dog* (to paraphrase the lengthy original title), a subject from Malory. He found oil painting difficult and, despite assistance from Brown and Rossetti, the picture was probably never completed. In any case, he must have put it aside in early August for this time marked the start of the Jovial Campaign to decorate the new extension to the Oxford Union building.

Rossetti had visited Oxford earlier in the year taking Morris with him as guide and general factotum. They had gone at the invitation of the architect of the new Science Museum, Benjamin Woodward, who wished to commission Rossetti to paint a mural. Hardly surprisingly, the subject, *Newton gathering pebbles on the shores of the Ocean of Truth*, failed to inspire Rossetti to anything but amusement. However, expansive and rash as ever, he offered to paint the interior of Woodward's newly completed Union debating chamber with subjects from Malory. He assured the Union Committee that the work could be carried out for the cost of materials and lodgings, and his offer was eagerly accepted.

Back in London, Rossetti set out to recruit a team of artists by beguiling and bullying. Morris and Jones would go, of course, and the nineteen-year-old Val Prinsep, a pupil of GF Watts, who professed inexperience, was persuaded by Morris's example. "Nonsense", said Rossetti, when Prinsep demurred, "There's a man I know who has never painted anything – his name is Morris – he has undertaken one of the panels and he will do something very good you may depend – so you had better come!". Eventually the expeditionary force included Arthur Hughes, JR Spencer-Stanhope and John Hungerford Pollen, an elderly artist with a fading reputation who Rossetti had befriended and championed.

The interior of the Debating Chamber offered particular difficulties to the painters. It was oval in shape with a high beamed roof and each of the ten rectangular bays above the gallery, on which they were to paint, was pierced by two circular, multifoil, Gothic windows. These not only interrupted the design but also, as the sole source of illumination, made the painted area seem particularly dark. In the event, the windows proved to be the least of their difficulties for they painted on unprepared surfaces with unsuitable materials and within years the murals had flaked and darkened. Morris, who in addition to his bay had painted the roof, provided new designs for it in 1875, gratis, which may still be seen.

The decoration was supposed to be completed in six weeks, but September came and went – and October – and the "bargain" was becoming a considerable expense to the Union Society. In October, the three moved to lodgings in George Street, presumably because the regular occupants of the High Street rooms had returned after the Long Vacation. It was from these new digs, one evening in early October, that Rossetti

right THE OXFORD UNION LIBRARY, DESIGNED BY BENJAMIN WOODWARD AND DECORATED BY ROSSETTI AND HIS MERRY BAND IN 1857. THE CEILING DESIGN WAS SUPPLIED BY MORRIS IN 1875 TO REPLACE HIS PREVIOUS WORK WHICH HAD DETERIORATED BADLY.

above THE CHAUCER
WARDROBE, DESIGNED BY
PHILIP WEBB AND PAINTED
BY EDWARD BURNE-JONES IN
1859-60 AS A JOINT WEDDING
PRESENT FOR WILLIAM AND
JANE MORRIS.

and Jones went to a makeshift theatre in Russell's Tennis Court, where
they probably saw a touring company perform *Ben Bolt*, a popular nau-
tical drama. There, in the gallery, they first set eyes on the 18-year-old
Jane Burden, the woman who was to marry Morris and love Rossetti. The
subject of William Morris's Union mural, *How Sir Palamedes loved La Belle
Iseult with exceeding great love out of measure, and how she loved not him again
but rather Sir Tristram*, was to prove sadly prophetic.

Jane was the third of the four children of Robert and Anne Burden. Her father was a stableman and her family was extremely poor. She and her younger sister Bessie, were educated at a Parish School, quite possibly that in Rose Lane, Oxford, where she would have learnt reading and writing in the mornings and, more practically for a girl of her class, destined to be a servant, needlework and ironing every afternoon. On Saturdays, the pupils were taught how to "scour" out a room. Her older brother William had become a College servant when he was 14 years old but Jane's occupation is not known. She was living at her parents' home, a diminutive cottage in Holywell Street, when they first saw her, and may have been temporarily unemployed or taking in needlework.

Her appearance was striking; she was a tall, pale-complexioned young woman, handsome rather than pretty, with large eyes under dark eyebrows, full curved lips, a long neck and masses of black curling hair. Both Rossetti and Jones were instantly smitten, for Jane Burden was an absolute "stunner".

Presumably the urbane Rossetti, an expert in accosting young women, invited her to sit for them and, presumably, Jane agreed subject to her parents' approval for, "They made interest with her family and she sat to them." She began by posing for Rossetti for Queen Guinevere but on 14 November, his mural still incomplete, he suddenly left Oxford for Matlock, in Derbyshire, where his long-suffering fiancée Elizabeth "Lizzie" Siddal was staying. Jane then sat for Morris for his only completed oil painting, *La Belle Iseult*, now in the Tate Gallery, London.

The gauche, shy Morris, unused to women other than those of his family, seems to have become infatuated with her almost immediately. The contrast between the suave and worldly Rossetti, experienced in seduction, extrovert, confident and amusing, and the awkward and inexperienced Morris must have made a deep impression upon Jane. His courtship was the source of much levity to his friends; Prinsep reported that Morris was wooing her by reading *Barnaby Rudge* aloud.

Morris stayed on in Oxford after Jones returned to London, struggling with his picture on which he is reported to have written – "I cannot paint you but I love you." Jane Burden's beauty inspired him to verse and he wrote several more poems to add to the collection which he hoped to publish under the title *The Defence of Guinevere*. The book was rejected by Macmillan but was subsequently published by Bell and Daldry, at Morris's own expense, in the following year, March 1858. He dedicated it to Rossetti.

In the early summer of 1858, Morris told Jones that he was engaged to Jane Burden. Algernon Swinburne wrote, excitedly but perhaps more perceptively than he knew, "The idea of marrying her is insane. To kiss her feet is the utmost man should dream of doing."

Years later, after Morris's death, Jane said that she had never loved Morris, but her agreement to marry him should come as no surprise and was neither wicked nor cynical. Any scruples she may have had were doubtless quashed by her family who certainly saw Morris as a future benefactor, a belief that proved to be justified, at least in part. For Jane, marriage to Morris meant financial security and social elevation of almost fairy-tale proportions. Morris's motives are much more problematic. There is no doubt that he was in love, but he was in love with La Belle Iseult not with an ill-educated, working class young woman from the back streets of Oxford.

His family, if he told them, would certainly have advised against such a match and true friends must have expressed their doubts. Perhaps he proposed in order to stress his independence, for he was a stubborn man; perhaps, again, as a rejection of his father's values. He may, of course, have been sufficiently naive as to feel obliged to marry her once he had started to woo her.

There is sufficient evidence to show that during 1858 he was more than usually pre-occupied and "Topsian". In January, when he must have been thinking of whether or not to offer marriage to Jane, Madox Brown recorded in his diary that "Jones is going to cut Topsy, he says his over-bearing temper is becoming quite insupportable as well as his conceite". Perhaps Morris doubted the strength of his feelings and the wisdom of his actions. It is also possible that he resented Jones's own engagement which must, of necessity, have altered their relationship. It is even possible that, unconsciously, he purchased her, a much admired and beautiful object, just as he had bought the *Morte d'Arthur* in Birmingham four years before, and had it bound in white vellum.

In August 1858, Morris made yet another tour of Northern France. Jones was unwell so he took as his companions Charles Faulkner and Philip Webb who had now left Street's office and set up on his own. During the tour, Morris and Webb discussed an ideal house, a house which Webb should design and Morris live in after his marriage. While Morris and his companions admired the noble ecclesiastical architecture of Picardy, Dante Gabriel Rossetti paid a short visit to Oxford where he drew a ravishing portrait, *Miss Jane Burden, aetat 18*.

Then, on 26 April 1859, William Morris, gentleman, married Jane Burden, spinster, in St Michael's Parish Church, Oxford. Most of The Set were present but Morris's family did not attend. Mrs Morris was to prove an excellent mother-in-law to Jane, but the prospect of their two families meeting socially was out of the question.

The marriage over, Mr and Mrs William Morris, Topsy and Janey to their friends, set off on their honeymoon travelling through France, Germany and the Rhineland.

right LA BELLE ISEULT, MORRIS'S PAINTING OF JANE BURDEN BEGUN AT OXFORD AND COMPLETED IN LONDON IN 1858-59.

THE RED HOUSE

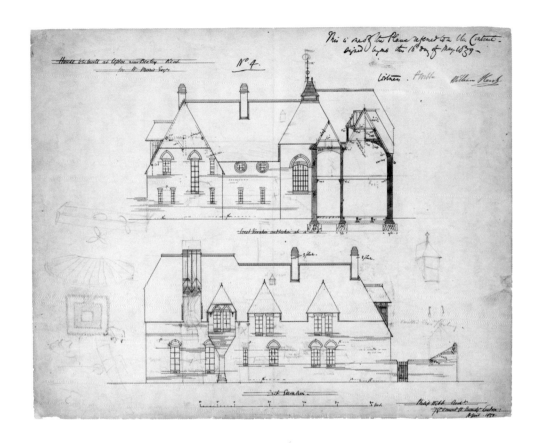

"The beautifullest place on earth."

EDWARD BURNE-JONES (1860)

IN THE DAMP AUTUMN OF 1858, William Morris and Philip Webb were searching for a site on which to build a house for Morris and Jane Burden who was soon to become his wife. Details of land for sale must have been sent to Red Lion Square and excursions made on horseback to those that seemed promising. The ascetic Webb encouraged the recalcitrant Morris to forego his lunch on these expeditions, the latter complaining, "It is all very well, but I shall starve". The site they finally chose was an orchard in the hamlet of Upton in Kent, abutting, much to Rossetti's delight, the rustically named Hog's Hole.

Although deep in the north Kent countryside, Upton had recently become far more accessible to London with the extension of the London and Greenwich Railway, and Abbey Wood station on the North Kent line was a mere three miles away. Apart from its convenience, the site had a further significance for Morris for it lay on the route of the ancient Watling Street, the path that Chaucer's Pilgrims took to Canterbury, a virtual ley-line for Morris who was to commemorate the association with Chaucer by naming the garden porch The Pilgrim's Rest.

Work began during the summer of 1859 when the newly-wed Morrises had returned from their honeymoon. After a brief period in furnished rooms in Great Ormond Street, Morris and Jane moved to Aberleigh Lodge, which neighboured the site, so that he could supervise the work and doubtless terrify the workmen. Twelve months later, the building was completed and the Morrises moved in.

The design of Red House, Webb's first commission, must have been collaborative. Morris, one suspects, provided the romantic elements and Webb interpreted these in a practical way. This combination of romance and rationality, medievalism and modernity was recognized by Rossetti, writing in 1862, "It is a most noble work in every way, and more a poem than a house, but an admirable place to live in too."

Morris considered it to be "mediaeval" but in doing so, was almost certainly referring to the feel and intention of the building rather than the style. Morris had no time for slavish imitations of past styles nor for "Gothick" pastiche. He correctly divined that architects who practised either of these failed to understand the fundamentals of medieval architecture. In his case, this may be summed up as truth to materials, fitness for function, integrity of ornament, simplicity and satisfaction in building. Red House was medieval in that it was built by local workmen from local materials, its construction was revealed, not hidden, and its outward form proclaimed its internal functions. These "mediaeval" qualities are identical to those which caused Nikolaus Pevsner, among others, to consider it the precursor of the modern movement.

Superficially, the exterior is Gothic. The great arched entrance porch, the high irregular roofs, the subtle patterns in the brickwork and, above

previous page left A FITTED SEAT IN THE ORIEL WINDOW IN THE RED HOUSE DRAWING ROOM. FROM THIS WINDOW, WHICH PROJECTS FROM THE WESTERN ELEVATION AT FIRST-FLOOR LEVEL, THERE WERE SPLENDID VIEWS OF THE ANCIENT ORCHARD AND THE SURROUNDING KENTISH COUNTRYSIDE.

previous page right PHILIP WEBB'S DESIGN FOR RED HOUSE, THE "MEDIAEVAL" HOUSE THAT WAS BUILT FOR MORRIS IN AN ORCHARD AT UPTON, KENT, IN 1860.

left MORRIS'S CARTOON FOR *ARTEMIS*,
ONE OF THE SERIES OF *ILLUSTRIOUS
WOMEN* WHICH WERE TO BE
EMBROIDERED FOR THE DINING ROOM
AT RED HOUSE.

all, the asymmetry of the L-shaped building set around the romantic cone-roofed central well are all features that became staples of the Victorian Gothic repertoire and appeared, debased, in many a city suburb. But the lightness and logic of the interior, dominated by the airy central stairwell at the hub of the two wings, is totally original and thoroughly practical.

"It was not a large house", wrote Georgiana Burne-Jones, "but purpose and proportion had been so skilfully observed in its design as to arrange for all reasonable demands and gave an impression of ample space everywhere." The house is smaller than it looks for the overall impression from the exterior is deceptive. Much of the mass of the building is provided by the steeply gabled roof; once inside, the rooms are surprisingly moderate in size, the largest being roughly 20 x 12 ft (6 x 3.6 m), not much bigger than those found in the gable-fronted Victorian terrace houses which spread, street after identical street, through the outer London suburbs.

There are four decent sized bedrooms with a further small one and a partitioned dormitory to house the cook and three maids. The latter are situated at the end of the western wing and reached by the back stairs which ascend from the kitchen, scullery and other domestic offices on the ground floor. Thus they form a virtually self-contained unit separated from the rest of the house.

Webb gave much thought to the windows, both aesthetically and practically. Round ones signify corridors, and each room has windows suited to its purpose. The largest illuminates the first floor drawing room which also has a projecting oriel in the west wall providing views over the fruit trees to the surrounding countryside. The beautiful but practical studio which Philip Webb designed for Morris, would be the envy of any writer, artist or designer. It is flooded with light as it is the only room lit from three directions.

Once the house was completed, Morris together with the willing complicity of Jones and with a perversity which can only be explained by wild and youthful enthusiasm, developed a decorative scheme for the house. Had it been completed, it would have completely destroyed the simple beauty of Webb's building.

Although Rossetti's interests were changing in 1860, returning to Dante, his first and last inspiration, Morris and Jones were at their most medieval. They were by no means alone in their admiration for the Middle Ages for "mediaeval" was by now a recognized Victorian style and the work of The Firm (which Morris was soon to found) was to be exhibited in the Medieval Court of the 1862 International Exhibition.

The two friends determined to decorate Red House as they imagined a thirteenth-century house would have been decorated and the media they chose were tempera and embroidery. The principal feature was the geometric ornament which was to be applied to ceilings, beams and doors. Patterns were pricked out in the wet plaster so that they could be re-painted when necessary, a sensible procedure in a house lit largely by candle-light and oil lamps which soon darkened painted surfaces.

The hall and staircase were to be painted with scenes from the Trojan Wars designed by Jones, one of which was to be "a great ship carrying Greek heroes". The ground floor dining room was to be hung with appliqué embroidered panels of *Illustrious Women* which were probably inspired by Chaucer's *Legend of Good Women*, although the characters were not identical.

The most elaborate scheme was reserved for the drawing room. Above the dado, which ran around the room from the great brick fireplace surmounted by the motto *Ars longa vita brevis*, Jones was to paint a frieze of individual pictures illustrating the fifteenth-century English romance *Sire Degrevaunt* directly onto the wall. The panelled dado itself was to be covered by an imitation hanging, painted on canvas by Morris, which was based upon his *Si je puis* embroidery, worked in 1859 at Red Lion Square. The motto was found elsewhere in the house: in the small quarries of painted glass designed by Webb which were set into some of the windows, and in the painted tiles which lined the main and garden porches. Other tiles were painted with the Morris coat of arms which he used at this time and no other, probably because of the chivalric associations of heraldry.

Lizzie Siddal began to decorate the principal bedroom with a scene from the Garden of Eden until illness forced her to abandon it. Eventually the room was hung with curtains of dark blue serge, embroidered in colourful wools with a daisy pattern discovered in a Froissart manuscript found by Morris in the British Museum.

Much of the furniture was also painted. Webb's vast settle stood, and stands today, at the far end of the drawing room. He added a charming, child-sized minstrel's gallery which was reached by a ladder from the floor and gave access to the roof space, through a small door set in the wall. The settle was decorated overall, but its outstanding feature was a set of three doors painted by Rossetti with scenes from Dante's *Vita Nuova*. He had begun them in 1859 but the central panel remains uncompleted. The side panels show the earthly and heavenly meetings of Dante and Beatrice and the unfinished one, now in the Tate Gallery, is an invention of Rossetti's, *Dantis Amor*, an angel holding a sundial between the profiled heads of Christ and Beatrice. Piling Ossa on Pelion, Jones began a painting from the Niebelungleid on the interior of one of these doors.

The Morris's bedroom housed the Chaucer wardrobe which had been

above A TILE FOR THE GARDEN PORCH OF RED HOUSE DECORATED WITH THE MORRIS ARMS, A HORSE'S HEAD BETWEEN THREE HORSESHOES, GRANTED TO MORRIS'S FATHER IN 1843.

decorated by Jones with the gory story of Little Sir Hugh of Lincoln. He and Webb, who had designed it, gave it to the Morris's as a joint wedding present. Morris himself was painting the entrance hall settle, an imposing but utilitarian piece designed by Webb, with a sloping roof to prevent dust gathering. Raymond Watkinson has suggested that the musicians Morris portrayed, against a background probably inspired by the wattle fences of the Red House garden, illustrate a scene at "Joyous Gard", the castle of Sir Lancelot.

The literary sources that inspired the decorative schemes are noticeably diverse: Greek, Chaucerian, Arthurian and Germanic. If we add Northern sagas, this is a combination which Morris was to use again in *The Earthly Paradise*, the vast narrative poem which was certainly conceived and probably begun during the Red House years.

With the exception of the bedroom hanging, none of the decorations was completed. Three of Jones's *Sire Degrevaunt* murals were painted and remain today, the last shows Morris and Jane as the King and Queen at a wedding feast. Eight of the *Illustrious Women* were embroidered, each 3 ft (92 cm) high and intended by Jones to be separated by formalized trees. Rossetti abandoned *Dantis Amor* and Morris left Joyous Gard unfinished. Commissions and commerce took priority and births and illnesses caused welcome and worrying diversions.

However, as at Oxford during the painting of the Debating Chamber, the cooperative execution of the work was delightful. Days at Red House in the early sixties were a combination of strenuous and concentrated activity with convivial meals and games, and both work and play were leavened by practical jokes and Morris-baiting. Nobody present ever forgot Morris's rage when he discovered that Rossetti was busy painting "As I can't" on the unfinished drawing room hanging, nor how quickly his anger evaporated.

Morris and Jane worked on the embroidery together taking apart ancient fragments to discover authentic techniques. She carried out the needlework with her sister Bessie and was sometimes helped by Georgie who had married Edward Burne-Jones on 9 June 1860. Quite when Jones added the Burne to his name is not known but George Boyce first uses the double-barrel in 1863 and he may have adopted it after his marriage, presumably to differentiate himself from other painting Joneses. To Morris, though, he always remained Ned Jones.

Morris and Jane were also responsible for stencilling the ceilings which must have been arduous and back-aching work, hard to reconcile with Jane's later frailty. Sometimes they were assisted by Charlie Faulkner who was a frequent guest. It was Faulkner who gave Morris a black-eye, a "shiner", with a well-aimed windfall apple lobbed from the Minstrels' Gallery and he may well have devised the subtle joke of

sewing a tuck in Morris's waistcoat so that he was unable to fasten the buttons and thought that he had put on even more weight.

Red House was full of young people in 1860 for Morris was only 26 years old, Janey a mere 21, and Georgie a year younger. The wonderful new house, The Towers of Topsy as Rossetti called it, was a haven for all their friends and Morris presided over them all with great hospitality and only the occasional explosion.

Most of the decoration was carried out during the latter part of 1860 and daily life there during this period was vividly recalled by Georgiana Burne-Jones when she wrote her husband's *Memorials* in 1904. Ned and

above DANTIS AMOR, THE UNFINISHED CENTRAL PANEL FOR THE DOORS OF PHILIP WEBB'S GREAT SETTLE, PAINTED BY DG ROSSETTI IN 1859 AND 1860.

above A CARICATURE OF MORRIS FEEDING HIS TWO DAUGHTERS, JENNY AND MAY, BY BURNE-JONES.

Georgie were virtually permanent residents until late October; Faulkner and Webb, Rossetti and Lizzie were frequent guests, and the Madox Browns welcome visitors. Morris's mother must have driven over from Essex to see her eldest son's latest extravagance. She proved invaluable in recommending servants, including the coachman. A cook was certainly employed together with at least one live-in maid, other help for cleaning and gardening was doubtless obtained locally.

Weekend guests usually arrived on Saturdays, having been given written instructions about the train times from London Bridge. If they were fortunate, they would be met at Abbey Wood station by Morris's medieval wagonette, with leather curtains and his coat of arms emblazoned on the back. After the short but bumpy journey to Upton, the sound of the iron shod wheels upon the gravel drive of Red House would bring Morris, Jane or both to greet them under the great arch of the entrance porch.

Dinner was a moveable feast, sometimes eaten at midday and sometimes in the evenings when "It was the most beautiful sight in the world to see Morris coming up from the cellar before dinner, beaming with joy, with his hands full of bottles of wine and others tucked under his arms." Meals were served at a long plain table although they would certainly have been given plenty of linen napery as wedding presents. The lack of a tablecloth at the Morris's struck George Bernard Shaw as being novel as late as the 1880s. In the 1860s, it was revolutionary but had both collegiate and medieval connotations for Morris.

The glasses used by Morris were designed by Philip Webb. Some, like the wine glasses, were simple and unadorned in pale greenish glass, but other pieces – decanters and large beakers – were decorated with applied knops and raised rings, like German glass of the seventeenth century. The silver cutlery was probably a gift from Mrs Morris.

If they had porcelain plates they were not often used. The Morris's and their friends had a passion for Staffordshire blue and white, a craze that seems to have been started by the Madox Browns, probably in their case because of relative poverty. "At their table the standard of the common English Willow-pattern plate was boldly raised", wrote Georgie, "in spite of Gabriel's enquiries for it at a china shop having been met with insult by the proprietress." In the same year, 1860, Lizzie Siddal ended a letter to Georgie "with a Willow pattern dish full of love to you and Ned." Later, when all were richer, Rossetti and Whistler competed in acquiring the finest oriental blue and white china, and Morris too bought many excellent pieces.

There is sadly no record of the food served at Red House but from what we know of Morris in later years dinner would have been incomplete without a large joint of roast beef, lamb or mutton. The meal would end with dessert, apples and pears from the orchard, accompanied by port, a drink that the gout-prone Morris reluctantly eschewed in later life. When only close friends were present, a favourite joke was to send Morris to Coventry, only communicating with him via Jane.

The evening meal was sometimes followed by a game of hide-and-seek which must have been great fun in a house still crammed with the paraphernalia of decorating. If less active entertainment was desired, Georgie would sing, accompanying herself on the piano – "She is pretty", wrote Mrs Bell Scott shortly after meeting her, "a very little creature, indeed, and sang the ballad of 'Green sleeves' and others in loud wild tones quite novel and charming."

Mornings at Red House were spent on practical activities. The men would paint and the women sew or, in Georgie's case, practice cutting wood blocks. If the weather was fine, Janey and Georgie would take their work outdoors and sit at a solid red table in the shelter of the porch which overlooks the picturesque well. From here they could watch the progress of the garden which Webb and Morris had designed together.

Features of the garden appear in Webb's plans and elevations, for the house and garden were designed as one, a practice he was to continue for the rest of his career. At the front of the house, enclosed by the semi-cir-

right THE ASCENSION STAINED-GLASS WINDOW DESIGNED BY WILLIAM MORRIS FOR THE CHURCH OF ALL SAINT'S, SELSEY, IN 1863.

cular drive which ran from the entrance gate, past the front door and thence to the stable, Morris planned a formal garden. This took the form of a square made up of four smaller square plots separated from each other by narrow paths. Each small square was fenced with rustic hurdles of woven branches and the overall effect was like an illustration to a medieval *Book of Hours*.

The grassed area which surrounded the wellhouse was enclosed on its two open sides by a tall wooden trellis against which climbing roses were planted. This trellis, together with the walls of the house, formed the boundary of a grassed rectangular courtyard of roughly 20 x 40 ft (6 x 12 m). The walls of the house were planted with climbers which are clearly indicated on Webb's drawings of the Red House.

Mackail recorded that Morris justifiably prided himself on his knowledge of gardening and garden design. He had loved plants since his boyhood at Woodford Hall and they were to inspire almost all his future designs. As the garden matured, fruit, flowers and vegetables were to be had in abundance, the scented roses covered the trellises and the flowering creepers scaled the lofty walls.

Afternoons were for leisure. Jane, Georgie and other guests, sometimes accompanied by Morris, explored the neighbouring countryside by foot or pony, or made longer excursions in the wagonette. Burne-Jones never went with them, he hated the country except, as he told his father, for the apples. He was more likely to be found playing skittles on the bowling green cleared from the orchard at the side of the long western elevation of the house.

Looking back in the early years of the twentieth century, these days of quiet work and boisterous leisure, country walks and impromptu concerts lit by the glow of oil lamps and the sweetly scented apple logs blazing in the great brick fireplace of the drawing room, seemed to Lady Burne-Jones to be ones of pre-lapsarian innocence and happiness.

On 17 January 1861 Janey gave birth to her first daughter Jane Alice, known as Jenny. Madox Brown's wife Emma stayed with her as help and companion and Mrs Morris found Elizabeth Reynolds to be the child's nurse. So many guests attended Jenny's christening party, that the drawing room had to improvise as a dormitory for the men. Swinburne, being the smallest, was given the sofa. Later in the year, in October, Philip Burne-Jones was born, but rejoicing was tinged with sadness for between these two birthdays the Rossetti's had suffered a tragedy.

Rossetti had first met Lizzie Siddal in September 1850. Her most striking feature was her golden-red hair: John Ruskin described her as "as beautiful as the reflection of a golden mountain in a crystal lake". They became "engaged" in 1852 and by 1854 she was Rossetti's pupil as well as being his fiancée and his muse. Their relationship was seldom happy,

however, as Rossetti was unfaithful and Lizzie suffered much from unspecified illnesses. Apart from his visit to Matlock during the painting of the Oxford Union they were estranged between July 1858 and the spring of 1860 when, convinced that she was dying, Rossetti married her in Hastings.

By the time they married she was almost certainly addicted to sleeping draughts which may have contributed to the death of her stillborn daughter on 2 May 1861. In July, she convalesced at Red House but her health, both mental and physical, never recovered and she committed suicide with an overdose of laudanum on 11 February 1862, just over a month before the birth of the Morris's second daughter Mary, known as May.

above THE DAISY HANGING DESIGNED BY MORRIS AND EMBROIDERED BY JANE MORRIS AND HER SISTER BESSIE BURDEN FOR THE BEDROOM AT RED HOUSE IN 1860.

The building and decorating of Red House had been paid for out of Morris's income from his shares. By the age of 25, Morris had never earned a penny for *The Defence of Guinevere* had been coolly received and had not recouped the cost of publication. So far as his worried mother was concerned, he was a failed cleric, failed architect, failed painter and failed poet, but in 1861 Morris was to find employment.

George Boyce's diary entry of 26 January reads, "Jones told me he and Morris and Rossetti and Webb were going to set up a sort of shop where they would jointly produce and sell painted furniture." The friends must have discussed the practicalities of the venture during late 1860 and plans were well advanced by the time Burne-Jones told Boyce.

By April they had acquired premises above a jewellery manufacturer at 8 Red Lion Square, a stone's throw from their old lodgings. On 11 April they published a circular which stated their aims and the services on offer. The tone of this manifesto is remarkably arrogant for a fledgling enterprise and betrays the hand of Rossetti, confident and optimistic as ever.

The Firm that the friends set up together was called Morris, Marshall, Faulkner and Co. – Fine Art workmen in Painting, Carving, Furniture and the Metals. The partners were Morris, Burne-Jones, Rossetti, Webb, Madox Brown, Faulkner and Peter Paul Marshall. The latter was a friend of Brown's, a qualified surveyor and sanitary engineer and a keen amateur painter. It seems probable that Arthur Hughes considered joining them but finally refused. Each partner contributed a £1 share to the working capital and Morris's mother made an interest free loan of £100.

According to their advertisement, "These artists having been for many years deeply attached to the study of the Decorative Arts of all time and countries, have felt more than most people the want of some one place where they could either obtain or get produced work of a genuine and beautiful character", and it goes on to list work that they were willing to undertake. These were mural decoration in "pictures or in pattern", architectural carving, stained glass, metalwork and jewellery, plain, carved or painted furniture and "embroidery of all kinds".

The list is revealing for it shows, first, how much they were utilizing the experience of decorating and furnishing Red House. Second, it indicates a recognition that although they hoped to gain domestic commissions, the ecclesiastical market was most likely to provide them with lucrative work. One of the first items that the partners purchased was a Clergy List.

The first year must have been largely spent in creating work for stock because they may well have already decided that the International Exhibition to be held in South Kensington in 1862 would provide them with an excellent opportunity to bring their work publicity. They took two stands in the Medieval Court of the Exhibition, one for stained glass and one for furniture and embroidery, and their investment proved to be successful for they were awarded two medals and sold over £150 of work, including the St George cabinet, designed by Webb and decorated by Morris, which is now in the Victoria and Albert Museum.

Their glass was unpopular with other manufacturers who accused them of incorporating pieces of original medieval work but its superior quality was immediately recognized by architects. The exhibition brought them several important commissions, most notably from the Gothic Revival architect GF Bodley who ordered windows for his new churches St Michael and All Angels, Brighton, and All Saints, Selsey, in Gloucestershire. He also ordered glass, embroideries and decorative work for St Martin's, Scarborough and All Saints, Cambridge. After the Exhibition, the jubilant Morris entertained the partners and all the staff, a dozen or so men and boys under the foremanship of George Campfield, at Red House.

Despite the commissions, the finances of The Firm were rocky. It had been severely under-capitalized when it was founded and by the end of December 1862, Morris had advanced £400 and his mother had made a further loan of £200. As the business manager, Morris received a salary of £150 a year. The company would not become profitable for another four years, helped in part by the sale of Morris's wallpapers, the first of which,

overleaf MORRIS, WHO DISLIKED FORMALITY, ENJOYED PICNICS THROUGHOUT HIS LIFE AND PRIDED HIMSELF ON HIS SALADS. BOWLS, PLAYED IN THE ALLEY WHICH RAN UNDER THE WESTERN WALL OF THE HOUSE, WAS PARTICULARLY POPULAR DURING THE RED HOUSE YEARS.

"Daisy" and "Trellis", he designed in 1862 and printed in 1864.

In these early years, The Firm was as much a Brotherhood as a commercial enterprise. It was a Sisterhood, too, for Janey and Bessie embroidered, Georgie and Faulkner's sisters Kate and Lucy painted tiles and other friends and relations were called upon when willing hands were needed. The partners met regularly, "once or twice a fortnight" according to Charlie Faulkner, who described the meetings as having "rather the character of a meeting of the 'Jolly Masons' or the jolly something elses than of a meeting to discuss business. Beginning at 8.00 for 9.00 pm. they open with the relation of anecdotes which have been culled by members of the firm since the last meeting – this store being exhausted Topsy and Brown will perhaps discuss the relative merit of the art of the thirteenth and fifteen century, and then perhaps after a few more anecdotes business matters will come up about 10 or 11 o'clock and be furiously discussed till 12, 1 or 2."

However, life at Red House could not be the same now that Morris was fully involved in his work for The Firm. Even weekends were less relaxed. William Allingham went down on a summer Sunday in 1864 – "By steamer to London Bridge and rail to Plumstead; after some wandering found the Red House at last in its rose garden, and William Morris and his queenly wife crowned with her own black hair." On the Monday he rose early and at 7.30, "We hurry to train. W.M. brusque, careless with big shoon." William Morris had become a commuter.

Janey must have felt the change more than Morris who at least had his work to absorb him and saw his friends every day. Stuck in the Kent countryside with her needlework she must at times have felt "aweary, aweary" like Tennyson's Mariana in the moated grange. Of course, friends still came to stay. The Burne-Jones's were there in May 1864 with their two-year-old son Philip who "shared the nursery of the Misses Morris, two beautiful children by this time."

Perhaps it was during this visit that the friends discussed the possibility of moving The Firm to Upton and building an extension to Red House as a home for Ned and Georgie. The idea almost became a reality, for Webb drew up plans which show a new wing, built along the line of the rose trellis, which would have formed a third side to the well court. If executed it would have been disastrous for the enclosed space would have been dark and damp and the shadow of the new building would

above A CORNER OF THE GARDEN AT RED HOUSE.

right A VIEW OF THE CONICALLY ROOFED WELL HOUSE WITH THE LARGE WINDOWED STAIR TOWER OF RED HOUSE BEYOND IT. THE SMALL CIRCULAR WINDOWS, WHICH MAY BE SEEN BEHIND THE LEAD FINIAL, DENOTE AN INTERNAL CORRIDOR.

have plunged much of Red House into darkness. It is hard to imagine that Morris and Webb did not realize this, but perhaps the former was desperate to have his old friends with him and perhaps the latter knew that it would never come to fruition.

In the late summer of 1864, the Morris and Burne-Jones families holidayed at Littlehampton with Faulkner and his sisters and on their return to London Philip Burne-Jones caught scarlet fever which he passed to Georgie who was then in the last weeks of pregnancy. The child, Christopher, weakened by her illness, only survived for three weeks and Georgie went to convalesce in Hastings.

Morris too was ill, confined to bed with rheumatic fever, when Ned wrote to him to say that he could not afford to move to Upton, a letter which reduced Morris to tears. The extension was abandoned and in the autumn of the following year the Morrises left Red House, never to return. Mackail states that Morris could no longer bear the cold Kent winds and that the move to London was made for reasons of health, but this is hardly convincing since the arrival of Ned and Georgie as neighbours, which he had argued keenly for only months before, would hardly have affected the weather.

Some subsequent biographers have claimed that the move was made from financial necessity, but in 1865 Morris's income from the dividends of his shares in Devon Great Consols was higher than it had been since 1857. The reason for the move seems to have arisen directly from the collapse of his plans to extend Red House for Burne-Jones. The latter's reluctance to move to Upton may have been due to poverty but as there is every reason to suppose that much of the financial burden would have fallen on Morris there may have been other reasons.

Both Georgiana Burne-Jones and JW Mackail wrote their accounts of life at Red House when Jane Morris was still alive and so were necessarily discreet; could Jane have demanded the move back to London? There is reason to believe that by 1864 Morris knew that Jane did not love him and evidence, admittedly ambiguous, in May's recollection that the Chaucer wardrobe had stood in "Mother's bedroom" at Red House, which suggests that they were no longer sleeping together. Perhaps the invitation to their old friends Ned and Georgie to join them at Upton was intended to mend matters between William and Jane, an attempt to return to the carefree days of 1860. The reason for the Burne-Jones's refusal might have been that they were all too aware of the role that had been allotted them.

Once the scheme had foundered, London, with its wider social possibilities, must have seemed extremely attractive to Jane. So the stoical Morris, putting her needs before his, reluctantly agreed to sell his beloved Red House and return to the hateful metropolis.

left "TRELLIS", THE SECOND WALLPAPER DESIGNED BY MORRIS IN 1862. IT WAS SUPPOSEDLY INSPIRED BY THE ROSE TRELLIS WHICH BORDERED THE WELL COURT AT RED HOUSE; THE BIRDS WERE DRAWN BY WEBB.

QUEEN SQUARE

"For this long time past I have, as it were, carried my house on my back"

WILLIAM MORRIS TO AGLAIA CORONIO
(FEBRUARY 1873)

WILLIAM AND JANEY MORRIS, THEIR TWO daughters and Aunt Bessie Burden moved into 26 Queen Square, Bloomsbury, in November 1865. Bessie had joined them on the death of her father some months earlier. Looking after Bessie was a practical example of Morris's duty as the Burden family's benefactor, but her skilful needle-work was an asset and she was a companion for Jane. Morris found her dull, but he was not alone in this for May recalled no childhood memories of her and although Bessie accompanied them on social occasions nobody thought to record anything about her but her presence – perhaps she was simply over-awed.

The Queen Square House had not been acquired simply to house the Morrises, it was needed to provide larger premises for The Firm which had out-grown Red Lion Square. Between Midsummer 1865 when the lease was signed and the beginning of 1870 Morris, Marshall, Faulkner & Co. was to be transformed. In 1865 it still owed substantial sums to Morris and his mother and financially went from crisis to crisis, but five years later it was truly established as a sound and responsible business. The man who achieved this was George Warington Taylor who joined the Company as business manager on 3 March 1865, at a salary of £120 a year. Taylor was a thirty-year-old consumptive, "a tall, thin man with a very large Roman nose", according to Georgie. He was an Old Etonian whose misfortunes had reduced him to working as an usher at Her Majesty's Theatre before being introduced to the partners by Rossetti.

Although he was incapable of running his own affairs, Taylor proved to be an excellent and efficient manager who brought order to chaos and replaced profligacy with prudence. He rapidly discovered that Morris was both too generous and too ill-organized and set about imposing a more rigorous approach to the business. He also realized, for he was a shrewd judge, that Morris admired people who stood up to him and adopted a bullying but affectionate manner towards his employer. He was particularly robust when discussing Morris's personal expenditure, "It is no use your blasting anybody's eyes – you must haul in." But although he adopted a tyrannical attitude, he was a kind and sympathetic man and the first to assist any worker who had fallen ill or needed help. He suited the Partners well and they suited him for he was an educated and cultivated man with a good knowledge of the arts.

Because of his consumption, Taylor lived in Hastings from 1867 until his early death in February 1870 and conducted much of his work by correspondence. It was in Sussex that he discovered two old chairs, a reclining arm-chair and a simple, rush seated chair, which when refined by Webb became The Firm's best-selling furniture, suitable for slimmer purses and smaller houses than the painted "mediaeval" pieces of the early years. Stained glass remained the Company's most profitable mer-

previous page left NUMBER 26 QUEEN SQUARE IN THE EARLY TWENTIETH CENTURY. MORRIS AND HIS FAMILY OCCUPIED THE UPPER FLOORS FROM 1865 UNTIL 1873 LIVING, LITERALLY, ABOVE THE SHOP.

previous page right THE BARD AND PETTY TRADESMAN, A CARICATURE OF MORRIS BY ROSSETTI DRAWN AFTER THE SUCCESS OF MORRIS'S EPIC POEM THE EARTHLY PARADISE IN 1868. MORRIS HABITUALLY WORE A BLUE FRENCH SMOCK WHEN WORKING.

chandise until the 1870s, but the ecclesiastical bias of the Company was diminishing and the number of domestic clients growing.

In 1866, The Firm received two important commissions to decorate the Tapestry Room and Armoury at St James's Palace and the new Dining Room at the South Kensington Museum. The former, which was extremely prestigious, arose from Rossetti's friendship with William Cowper-Temple, the First Commissioner for Works, and led to further decoration at the Palace in 1880. The commission for the Dining Room, which may still be visited in the Victoria and Albert Museum, resulted from their display at the 1862 Exhibition when the Museum had purchased stained glass. These enterprises established a place for Morris, Marshall, Faulkner & Co. among the leading firms of Interior Decorators.

Number 26 Queen Square was a large Queen Anne townhouse. The ground floor was given over to workshops and a shop where the products were displayed. Further manufacturing took place in the ballroom, a later addition to the house which had been built at the rear of the back courtyard and was reached from the main building by a glassed-in walkway (a studio for the glass painters). The Morris family and their three servants lived on the floors above. The grandest room in the house was the first floor drawing room which extended across the whole frontage and was lit by five tall windows overlooking the Square. The room was painted white, a significant departure from the "mediaeval" decoration of Red House yet equally revolutionary in 1865. The nursery was papered with "Trellis" with its bright birds and rural associations.

Jenny and May were probably too young to miss the gardens and orchards of Red House. All the greenery they saw was in the London squares and the grounds of Gray's Inn where Philip Webb had rooms, "a green secluded refuge, into the silence of which one literally plunged out of the grime and turmoil and rattle of Theobalds Road." May recalled tea with the dryly humorous Webb as "unalloyed bliss", jokes and jam and more jam and pictures.

The lack of a garden for the children was compensated for by frequent visits to Morris's mother at Leyton where she lived in "a fine square, spacious building set in well-bushed grounds, with a wide terrace lawn, and garden sloping to a wilderness." Here the children stayed for weekends or longer among "young aunts and uncles and first and second cousins... The family servants were also our playmates in leisure moments. They were of the old school, of course, affectionate and upright and intelligent, 'knowing their place'." The Butler "who had at once such a sense of decorum and of humour" told May and Jenny of how, when their father and Burne-Jones had dined at Mrs Morris's in Red Lion Square days their jokes had so amused him that he had to dash from the room to burst with laughter.

"I thank God my lot has been cast amidst you fellows for the end of my life would not have been pleasant without"

GEORGE WARINGTON TAYLOR
TO PHILIP WEBB

When Morris stayed with his mother nowadays there was more gravitas. As the oldest son, he would read family prayers to the assembled household on Sunday mornings before "the urn sizzles, the little dog patters in, sneezing with affection, and people sit down to breakfast." Morris, who had benefitted from his mother's kindness and largesse until well into his twenties, was a model son as he grew older, visiting her and writing to her regularly and sending her presents of claret and champagne. In 1871, Mrs Morris moved to The Lordship, a house at Much Hadham in Hertfordshire but the visits continued and the children often stayed for several weeks at a time when their parents were away. On occasion, Grandma would visit Queen Square, "in a carriage laden with fruit and flowers and all the country offerings so dear to Londoners", and take the children shopping and spoil them with sweets and treats as grandmothers are supposed to do.

There were many dinners at Queen Square in the first few years and from May's recollections they appear to have taken place in the drawing room. "I can well remember the look of the stately five-windowed room, with the long oak table laid for one of these dinners. What specially attracted my attention was not the old silver and blue china, but the greenish glass of delicate shapes, designed by Philip Webb and made for The Firm by Messrs Powell at the Whitefriars Glassworks. This gleamed like air-bubbles in the quiet candle-light and was reflected far away in the little mirrors set in the chimney-piece." May Morris was to use this glass for the rest of her life and on her death she left much of it to Birmingham Art Gallery.

One particularly memorable party was held to celebrate the publication of the first volume of *The Earthly Paradise* in May 1868. It was one of the very rare formal dinners given by Morris when guests were expected to wear evening dress, "togs". Quite who assisted the stout, untidy and irascible host with his studs and formed a seemly bow from the long white tie is not known. Sixteen guests sat down to dinner according to Allingham; Georgie and Ned Burne-Jones, Emma and Madox Brown and their daughter Lucy, Wilfred Heeley and his sister, the publisher FS Ellis and his wife, Mr and Mrs Charles Augustus Howell, George Boyce, Kate Faulkner, Bessie Burden and Dante Gabriel Rossetti. It was Allingham who christened the meal The Earthly Paradise and Burne-Jones who inscribed the title on his menu card. Years later May Morris wrote, "Like many other social functions of the kind it seems to have been rather dull according to the account of those of the party who have described it to me". But on this occasion she was certainly and deliberately misled.

At the time of the dinner she and Jenny were probably engrossed in their new pets, two young dormice which had arrived a couple of weeks earlier accompanied by a note from the donor – "I know you will take great care of them and always give them anything they are fond of – that is, nuts, apples and hard biscuits. If you love them very much I dare say they will get much bigger and fatter and remind you of your papa and me. Your affectionate D.G.Rossetti." The kind Mr Rossetti was in love with their mother.

The Earthly Paradise had pre-occupied Morris since 1865. Georgie recalled that on her final visit to Red House in the September of that year, her husband and Morris could talk of little else. It was originally conceived as a collaboration between them which Morris would write and Burne-Jones illustrate. This was still their intention in the following August when Allingham dined with them and Morris, "learned about wine and distilling", talked of *The Big Story Book*, as it was commonly called. It was to be in one large folio volume illustrated with 500 woodcuts and Morris intended to publish it at his own expense. Later the same month, Allingham joined the friends in Winchester. The party visited the cathedral where "Morris talked copiously and interestingly on all things". He declined the Verger's offer of a conducted tour, "and the Verger listened with the rest of us", on their return to Lymington, where they were staying, "M. being hot wants to sit in a draught." The next day they went on the beach and buried Morris up to his head in shingle. It was during this holiday that Ned teased Topsy by pretending that he had completed no more designs for *The Big Story Book*.

In fact, Burne-Jones produced about 70 drawings for *The Story of Cupid and Psyche* in 1865 and then a further 20 for *The Hill of Venus* by 1867. As usual Morris, who believed anybody could do anything if only they put their minds to it, turned to family and friends to cut the wood blocks from Ned's designs. Bessie did at least one and George Wardle, who was later to manage The Firm, was asked to do others. Soon, however, Morris, probably impatient, was doing the work himself and completed 35 blocks before the project was finally abandoned for technical reasons.

During 1866 there were regular dinners at Queen Square to discuss the book's progress and Morris would read his latest verses in "a full, slightly monotonous voice", as Edmund Gosse described it. Listening to Morris was not an unalloyed pleasure, even the loyal Georgie confessed to having to pinch herself on occasion in order to stay awake. Like

above JANE MORRIS, POSED BY ROSSETTI AND PHOTOGRAPHED BY JOHN PARSONS IN THE GARDEN OF TUDOR HOUSE, CHEYNE WALK, ON 5 JULY 1865.

Topsy's hair, the book grew and grew and Rossetti fantasized about a secret room at Queen Square filled to bursting with Morris's manuscript. The enormous poem owes an acknowledged debt to Chaucer's *Canterbury Tales* being a series of tales told by Northern mariners in search of the Earthly Paradise, and the Elders of an outpost of ancient Greek civilization who entertain them when they fail to find it. There are 24 tales in all, taken by Morris from Greek myth and Northern legend. One tale, *The Life and Death of Jason*, which was originally intended for the book, outgrew its role and was published separately in 1867 at Morris's expense. *Jason* sold well and the publishers, Bell and Daldry were happy to bear the cost of the second and subsequent impressions. When the first volume of *The Earthly Paradise* appeared in 1868 it was eagerly awaited, praised by the critics and purchased in great numbers by the public. From now on, Morris was known as a major poet to his contemporaries, quite literally *The Bard and Petty Tradesman* of Rossetti's caricature.

In October 1862, eight months after Lizzie's death, Rossetti settled in Tudor House, 16 Cheyne Walk, an imposing eighteenth-century building facing the Thames and overlooking Chelsea reach. He lived there in considerable and profligate style surrounded by his antique furniture and circular convex mirrors.

In summer, he erected an exotic marquee in the large rear garden. It was a pavilion fit for Sardanapalus or Kublai Khan, where guests reclined on Persian cushions and conversation was interrupted by the harsh shrieks of his peacocks. During his first five years at Tudor House Rossetti assembled a considerable menagerie; dormice, woodchucks, owls, salamanders, marmosets, armadillos and his beloved wombat had the freedom of his house while the buffalo, deer and kangaroos roamed the garden. Friends had to dissuade him from buying a lion and an elephant. The latter, he told a startled Browning, could clean his windows and thus attract the attention of any potential customer passing by. Few of the animals lived long: the Wombat, immortalized in verse and caricature, died within months. Although he was invariably in debt, constantly complaining of a lack of "tin", he entertained lavishly and kept a large and changing staff under the chaotic supervision of Fanny Cornforth, his model and mistress who, for propriety's sake, lived nearby in lodgings rented by Rossetti.

On 5 July 1865, before her departure from Red House, Jane Morris sat for John Parsons, a photographer, in the garden of Tudor House in attitudes posed by Rossetti. These photographs (one of them is reproduced on page 65) have a magical poignancy for Jane never smiles but looks melancholy, wistfully yearning for what might have been. Rossetti was to use them time and again in his work, they formed a matrix or virtual armature for the occasions on which she posed in person. The first of

left MRS WILLIAM MORRIS IN A BLUE DRESS, THE PORTRAIT OF JANEY WHICH ROSSETTI PERSUADED MORRIS TO COMMISSION IN 1868.

these seems to have taken place in early 1868 when Rossetti persuaded Morris to commission a portrait of his wife. Sittings began in March and all necessary proprieties were adhered to. Morris or Bessie accompanied Jane and sometimes stayed the night at Cheyne Walk. Indeed, the work seemed almost collaborative, a happy union of sitter, patron and painter. But at the same time, Rossetti was painting her as *La Pia de Tolomei*, a tragic figure from Dante's *Purgatorio*, deserted, imprisoned and finally murdered by a tyrannical and neglectful husband.

The portrait of *Mrs William Morris in a blue dress* was completed within the year and hung in the drawing room at Queen Square. Rossetti inscribed it in Latin, "Jane Morris, A.D.1868, Painted by D.G.Rossetti. Famed for her poet husband and surpassingly famous for her beauty, now let her gain everlasting fame by my painting." By September, when the Morrises accompanied the Howells to Southwold for a late summer holiday, Jane and Gabriel were having a clandestine correspondence.

The American novelist Henry James saw Rossetti's portrait of Jane when he visited Queen Square for dinner early in 1869 and reported to his sister that it "was so strange and unreal that if you hadn't seen her you'd pronounce it a distempered vision, but in fact an extremely good likeness." His letter is worth quoting at length as it provides a rare outsider's view of the Morris household in Queen Square and how bohemian it appeared to a disinterested observer. "Oh ma chere, such a wife! Je n'en reviens pas – she haunts me still...imagine a tall lean woman in a long dress of some dead purple stuff, guiltless of hoops (or of anything else, I should say) with a mass of crisp black hair heaped into great wavy projections on each of her temples, a thin pale face, a pair of strange, sad, deep, dark Swinburnian eyes, with great thick black oblique brows, joined in the middle and tucking themselves away under her hair...a long neck, without any collar, and in lieu thereof some dozen strings of outlandish beads...After dinner Morris read us one of his unpublished poems... and his wife, having a bad toothache, lay on the sofa, with her handkerchief to her face. There was something very quaint and remote from our actual life, it seemed to me, in the whole scene: Morris reading in his flowing antique numbers a legend of prodigies and terrors; around us all the picturesque bric-a-brac of the apartment...and in the corner this dark silent mediaeval woman with her mediaeval toothache."

The appearance of the Morris family did seem strange and *outré* to others. Jane was laughed at in France, much to Morris's rage, and May recalled a beastly boy cousin who teased her and Jenny because of the oddness of their clothes. Morris must have had much to do with his wife's costume for he maintained that one of the two things women knew nothing of was how to dress, the other being how to cook! Jane's dresses flowed and revealed her natural shape and the bustle, corset and

The M's at Ems

crinoline were banished from her wardrobe. In the 1880s, the pair of them became involved in the Rational Dress movement which was to finally triumph over the whale-boned imprisonment of the female body. Morris himself had largely abandoned the formal attire of the Victorian gentleman during the 1860s. For work he adopted the loose blue smock of the French artisan and when he needed to appear rather smarter he wore short jacketed, waistcoated blue serge suits which gave him the appearance of a sea-captain. He seems to have been unsure of himself when visiting tailors, writing to Janey in 1870 -"I went yesterday to order myself some new clothes; but was so alarmed at the chance of turning up something between a gamekeeper and a methodist parson, that I brought away some patterns in my hand to show Webb." Later, during his experiments in indigo dyeing during the 1870s, he took to wearing dark blue shirts made from his own materials, and in the 1890s was persuaded by the advocacy of George Bernard Shaw to patronize Dr Jaeger's shop for hygienic woollen clothing.

In 1869, Jane appeared to be extremely ill and Morris was advised by their doctors to take her abroad, to the fashionable German spa town of Bad Ems, in the Rheinland. The exact nature of Jane's illness is still not known and probably never will be. The symptom most often described

above THE M'S AT EMS, ONE OF A SERIES OF CARICATURES SENT BY ROSSETTI TO JANE MORRIS WHILE SHE WAS TAKING A CURE AT THE SPA TOWN OF BAD EMS IN 1869.

was backache, but her regime at Bad Ems and the subsequent installation of a combined shower and douche at Queen Square suggests that her problems were gynaecological; if so, this would go some way to explain the reticence of her contemporaries. Whatever the reason, from now on Jane was usually cast in the role of invalid and, without suggesting that she was a valetudinarian, it was a role which it probably suited her to accept. Invalids needed frequent holidays in pleasant places, peace and quiet, solitude when necessary, rooms of their own and, perhaps more importantly, beds of their own – so far as unwanted sexual attentions were concerned invalidism provided a convenient and permanent headache. Her delicacy was taken for granted by her friends. Recalling a boisterous children's party at the Grange in 1873, Georgie Burne-Jones concludes her description "while Mrs. Morris, placed safely out of the way, watched everything from her sofa."

Morris and Janey left London in July and were not to return until mid-September. Morris was worried, bored and irritable during this enforced absence from work and friends in London. He was also short of money and had to ask Webb for a loan. Bad Ems was an expensive place to stay and the treatment cannot have been cheap; what was worse was that it appeared to be ineffective. There was some fishing to be had and rowing on the river but the food was poor and Morris had always preferred French wine. His mood cannot have been improved by a succession of letters from Gabriel to Janey, some of which contained brilliant caricatures of Morris. Most of them are affectionate, but one, *The Ms at Ems*, is distinctly cruel. It portrays a bored Jane in her bath plagued not only by the daily dosage of Spa water but also by her husband's interminable reading aloud from *The Earthly Paradise*; her pose is identical to that which he had used for *La Pia*.

Rossetti's letters to Jane are openly loving and invite Morris's complicity in their relationship, for "The more he loves you, the more he knows that you are too lovely and noble not to be loved: and, dear Janey,

above AGLAIA CORONIO, MORRIS'S FRIEND AND CONFIDANTE FROM 1870, THE YEAR IN WHICH SHE SAT TO ROSSETTI FOR THIS PASTEL DRAWING.

there are too few things that seem worth expressing as life goes on, for one friend to deny another the poor expression of what is most at his heart. But he is before me in granting this, and there is no need for me to say it. I can never tell you how much I am with you at all times."

While the Morrises were miserable in Ems, Rossetti was miserable in Scotland, at Penkill Castle, Ayrshire, the ancestral home of Alice Boyd. He was staying there with his old friend William Bell Scott and Miss Boyd, concerned about the state of his eyes and nervous and depressed. Scott, probably correctly, considered Rossetti's illness to be psychosomatic, brought on by his love for Jane. One macabre consequence of his obsession was the exhumation of a manuscript notebook of his poems which he had buried in the coffin of Lizzie Siddal, entwined in her golden hair. He now wished to publish a book of verse which would include those he had written recently with Jane as his inspiration. Aware that even he could not publicly broadcast his adulterous passion for a close friend's wife, he had to deceive the public into thinking that they were addressed to the dead Lizzie. On 31 August he wrote to his brother William, who was preparing the edition for publication, "I don't think dating throughout would do"; it was imperative that the love poems should appear to date from before Lizzie's death in 1862. The exhumation took place on 10 October.

Jane was no better in the spring of the following year and went to Hastings for the bracing sea air. Rossetti borrowed the nearby country cottage of his friend and patron Barbara Boudichon. Initially he stayed there with an American journalist, William Stillman, but after Stillman's departure in early April he was joined on 12 April by Jane who stayed there, with the occasional visit from her husband, until 9 May. They were together at Scalands when Rossetti's *Poems* appeared. His fears about their reception were unjustified, they went through seven impressions in the first year. The favourable review in the *Academy* was written by William Morris.

Morris's apparent complicity in and acceptance of the affair between Jane and Rossetti should be seen as a sign of strength rather than weakness. Years later, in 1886, in a letter to Philip Webb about the relationship between man and wife under Socialism, he wrote, "Here then is in brief my views - 1st. The couple would be FREE. 2. Being free, if unfortunately distaste arose between them they should make no pretence of its not having arisen. 3. But I should hope that in most cases friendship would go along with desire, and would outlive it, and the couple would still remain together, but always as free people." This of course is ideal, in 1870 there was no question of not making a pretence of a marital breakdown but Morris, intellectually at least, recognized Jane's need for freedom. In his maturity, he considered the average middle-class marriage to

be legalized prostitution, the "buying" of the wife by the husband, and he felt guilt about his own failure to satisfy Jane's emotional needs, he wanted her to be happy. However, although Morris's *amour propre* suffered from Jane's behaviour, his true emotions were engaged elsewhere for he too was in love with the wife of a friend, in his case it was Georgiana Burne-Jones.

After he had completed his biography of Morris in 1899, Mackail wrote to Aglaia Coronio to apologize for his account of "those stormy years of *The Earthly Paradise*...which must be excessively flat owing to the amount of tact that had to be used right and left". Mackail, it should be remembered was Georgiana's son-in-law. Edward Burne-Jones, a man who remained emotionally immature throughout his life, fell passionately in love with Marie Zambaco in 1867. She was a relation of the powerful Ionides family, expatriate Greek merchants who were major patrons of the Pre-Raphaelites and of The Firm. She had married a Dr Zambaco, a fellow Greek, but had become bored and returned from Paris to London in 1866 with two small children. The affair between the passionate flame-haired Marie and the smitten Ned was serious and nearly ended in tragedy for in 1869 she attempted suicide when he reneged on a promise to elope with her. Georgie was deeply hurt and depressed by her husband's infatuation and for a time left him, staying in lodgings in Oxford with her children. Morris was the confidant of both of them and although he helped Ned, who was often distraught, his real sympathy lay with Georgiana and he undoubtedly fell in love with her. As Rossetti was writing sonnets praising Janey's surpassing beauty her husband was penning desolate verses about his unrequited love for another woman. He spent many hours in 1870 meticulously and painstakingly making an illuminated hand-written book for her – *A Book of Verse* – which was truly a labour of love.

From 1870 onwards, Morris's marriage was one of convenience which gradually grew into a close and affectionate friendship. His work and her illnesses meant that they usually spent several months of the year apart and, after 1872 when they moved from Queen Square, Morris always kept some simple accommodation at his places of work. But for the moment, a convenient solution was needed to prevent a general and public scandal, for Rossetti was not a man to whom discretion came naturally. Edmund Gosse attended a party at the Madox Brown's house in Fitzroy Square in the winter of 1870 where Mrs Morris "in her ripest beauty, and dressed in a long unfashionable gown of ivory velvet, occupied the painting throne" and Gabriel squatted on a hassock at her feet. The opportunity arose in June 1871 when Dante Gabriel Rossetti and William Morris took a joint lease on Kelmscott Manor, near Lechlade in Gloucestershire, far removed from the eyes of London Society.

right A PAGE FROM THE MANUSCRIPT VOLUME *A BOOK OF VERSE* WHICH MORRIS WROTE AND ILLUMINATED FOR GEORGIE BURNE-JONES IN 1870. GEORGE WARDLE, FAIRFAX MURRAY AND BURNE-JONES HIMSELF ALSO CONTRIBUTED TO THE BOOK.

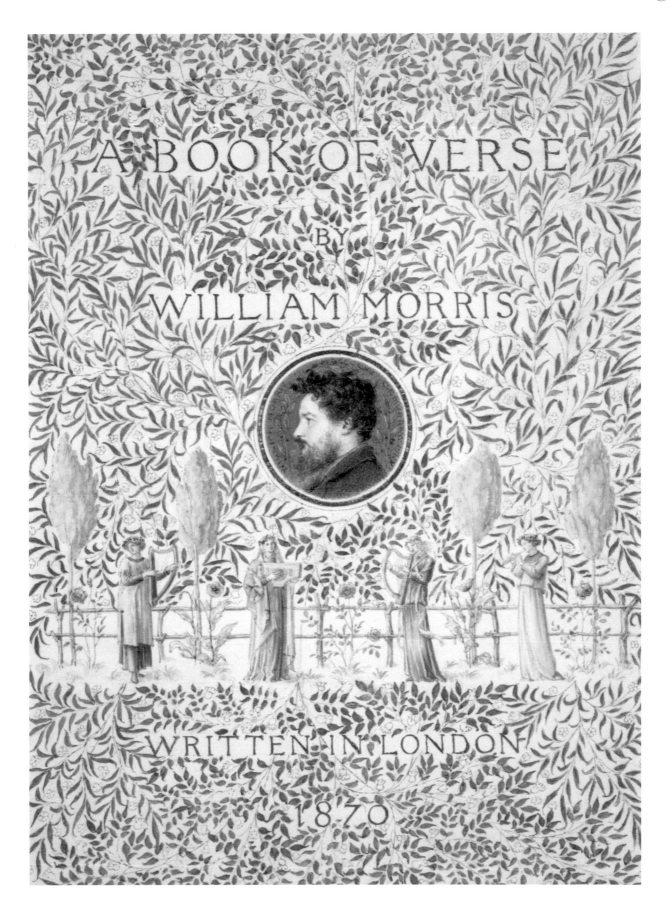

KELMSCOTT MANOR

"A house that I love with a reasonable love I think...so much has the old house grown up out of the soil and the lives of those that lived on it."

WILLIAM MORRIS

THE MOMENTOUS DISCOVERY OF KELMSCOTT MANOR on Tuesday 16 May 1871, was recorded by Charles Fairfax Murray, Morris's friend and occasional colleague, in a nondescript entry in his diary – "Breakfasted with Mr. Morris. Went with him to Faringdon, lunched at Lechlade and drove over to Kelmscott to look at a house and returned in the evening." For Morris it was "a heaven on earth", as he told Faulkner. Rossetti went down to see it a couple of days later and on 21 May they signed a joint lease at £75 per year. On 6 July, Morris, Jane and the children left London, the former bound for Iceland and the latter three for Kelmscott. Morris wrote to her that very evening, exhorting her to be happy and signing his letter, "Your affectionate William Morris", the only extant letter to her in which he does not send her his love. Ten days later Rossetti arrived at the Manor where the two lovers were to be alone for the next eight weeks.

Kelmscott Manor was "a perfect Paradise", Gabriel wrote to his friend Frederick Shields. The mellow, gabled building, concealed from the narrow, unmade road by a high lichened wall, had been built by 1571 for Richard Turner, a wealthy yeoman. The house was old-fashioned for its time and retained a medieval ground plan with kitchens and servants' quarters divided from the Great Hall and withdrawing rooms by an entrance passage contained between oak screens. The tall North-east wing which provides the house with its pleasing asymmetry was added in 1670 by Thomas Turner. The family was still prospering, Thomas had been granted a Coat of Arms in 1665 and, justifiably proud, had it carved and painted on a classical escutcheon between two plump harvest swags on his elegant new fireplace. Large stone barns surround the farmyard which lies to the left of the frontage and at the rear the garden and orchards fall away to the bank of the Upper Thames. The Manor stands apart from the village and is concealed from the approach road to Kelmscott, which runs through open fields, by a stand of trees. Morris and Rossetti rented the house from Elizabeth Turner who went to live nearby in her family farm after her husband's death in 1870.

To say that Jane and Gabriel were alone at Kelmscott is not quite true; Rossetti had taken two servants with him from Cheyne Row and, as he reported to his mother, there were also two "native" servants, the children's nurse and the children, "the most darling little self-amusing machines that ever existed." Jenny was ten and May a year younger and both were lively, observant and intelligent little girls. In the mornings, after watching Rossetti eat prodigious numbers of eggs, they were sup-

above A GREEN-PAINTED WASH-STAND, ONE OF THE FEW SURVIVING PIECES OF UTILITARIAN BEDROOM FURNITURE DESIGNED BY MADOX BROWN IN 1861.

right AN ATTIC BEDROOM UNDER THE SLOPING GABLE OF THE NORTH WING, WITH "BLACKTHORN" CURTAINS AND A SUSSEX CHAIR.

previous page left THE SIXTEENTH-CENTURY ENTRANCE PORCH TO KELMSCOTT MANOR, MORRIS'S BELOVED COUNTRY HOME FROM 1871.

previous page right KELMSCOTT TODAY.

posed to study under Jane's supervision but May was soon playing truant, messing about on the river in the punt or, even more dangerously, "roof-riding" on the ridges of the steeply pitched and high stone gables. On one occasion she became irretrievably stuck and the gardener, Philip Comely, was despatched to obtain the longest possible ladder.

Days were divided like the old Red House days, work in the mornings and leisure in the afternoons. For his studio, Gabriel used the Tapestry Room, hung with seventeenth-century scenes from the story of Samson, and he slept in the adjoining bedroom. He began painting immediately he had finished his breakfast and remained at work until dusk when he went for a solitary walk, rain or fine, and "returned after dark with a burden of weariness upon him."

But for the moment Rossetti was happy. He took other walks on the warm summer afternoons when the children were safely having tea with Mrs Turner and in these he was accompanied by Jane. She flourished under Gabriel's love and attention and was soon "taking five and six mile walks without the least difficulty." He was obviously proud of the effect he was having on her health and reported her achievements in a letter to Bell Scott - "Janey having developed a most triumphant pedestrian faculty, which licks you hollow, I can tell you." He was painting her, with the Thames and Manor in the background, for an intimate little picture called *Water-Willow*, and in the evenings, after the children had gone to bed, they read Shakespeare and Plutarch together and he may have given her a recently completed sonnet, inspired by her beauty.

On 16 September, William Morris returned from Iceland bringing

above left JENNY MORRIS, AGED 10, DRAWN IN PASTEL BY ROSSETTI AT KELMSCOTT MANOR IN 1871.

above right MAY MORRIS, AGED 9, A COMPANION TO THE PORTRAIT OF JENNY. MAY WAS A GREAT FAVOURITE OF ROSSETTI WHO OFFERED, IN JEST, TO ADOPT HER.

left WATER WILLOW, A HIGHLY PERSONAL AND INFORMAL PORTRAIT OF JANE MORRIS AT KELMSCOTT MANOR BY ROSSETTI. IT WAS PAINTED DURING MORRIS'S ABSENCE IN ICELAND IN 1871.

with him his Icelandic pony, Mouse, which became a great favourite of the children who had "a little basket-carriage, between the shafts of which he looked incredibly fat and funny." It would be wrong to think that Morris's journey to Iceland was a product of Jane's adultery but it was doubtless seen by all three of them as a temporary solution to an

impossible situation. Morris had discovered Iceland through its literature, particularly when he was writing *The Earthly Paradise*. In 1868, he was introduced by Warington Taylor to Eirikr Magnusson, an Icelandic scholar from whom he began taking lessons. A year later they published a translation of *The Story of Grettir*, quickly followed by their version of the *Volsunga Saga*. Magnusson, Faulkner and WH Evans, a friend of Faulkner's who wished to go for shooting and fishing, were Morris's companions on the Icelandic adventure. The expedition required considerable organization and Morris practised his cooking in the Burne-Jones's garden where, much to the amusement of their children, "he built a little hearth with loose bricks, over which he cooked a stew in the manner of some pirate or backwoodsman in a story book."

They sailed from Granton, a small fishing port on the Firth of Forth, on 8 July, bound for Reykjavik, the Icelandic capital, on a former gun boat named the *Diana*, decidedly crowded and none too clean. On the first morning of the voyage Morris "sat down to breakfast with a huge appetite (please don't be too much disgusted). Breakfast was beefsteak and onion, smoked salmon, Norway anchovies, hard-boiled eggs, cold meat, cheese and radishes and butter, all very plenteous... Faulkner looked serious as he sat down and presently disappeared." The next day Morris too was seasick.

The journey through Iceland, which Morris wrote up in a Journal for Georgie Burne-Jones, was enjoyable but arduous. They travelled by pony through a bleak and desolate landscape; across plains of black sand dissected by rushing crystal ice-cold streams, through gorges overhung with awesome jagged peaks and along narrow shaly tracks high on the

cliffs above the churning sea. In the evenings, they pitched camp in the meadows of hospitable homesteaders and bathed in the warm volcanic streams. The weather was often extreme with rain, sleet and snow and a wind "that cut like knives."

Morris had his usual misadventures, "to the great joy of my fellow travellers", and lost his pannikin strap, shortly followed by his pannikin, and his haversack, though all were returned by the kind and curious Icelanders. On Monday, 14 August, in the store at Olafsvik, they "bought some few horseshoes and I a sixpenny knife (for I had lost three)." Despite the hardships, Morris liked and admired many of the islanders he met and was moved to see the actual places where the mythical heroes of the Sagas had fought and schemed and caroused and sung. The physical dangers and mental demands of the journey purged him of much of his emotional despair. In November 1872, he wrote to Aglaia Coronio of his intention to return to Iceland in the coming year, for "I know clearer now than then what a blessing and help last year's journey was to me; what horrors it saved me from."

above and left JANE MORRIS'S BEDROOM AT THE MANOR. THE HANDSOME FOUR-POSTER BED HUNG WITH "WILLOW BOUGHS" CHINTZ WAS INHERITED FROM MORRIS'S PARENTS.

Rossetti was not immune from the horrors in 1872. His *Poems* had been attacked in the previous October by Robert Buchanan, writing under the pseudonym Thomas Maitland, in *The Contemporary Review*. What seems to have troubled Rossetti, who was already guilt-racked, in poor mental and physical health and by now addicted to the sleeping draught chloral, was that the article, *The Fleshly School of Poetry*, as its title suggests, criticized the morality of his work. Initially, he seemed to be unperturbed but it was probably one of the factors that brought about his total nervous collapse on 2 June 1872; six days later he attempted suicide. His friends, who were anxious to avoid a scandal, bustled the confused Gabriel off to Scotland and by 23 September, ignoring their entreaties and advice, he returned to Jane Morris and Kelmscott.

Morris took care to keep away. Although he had found it possible to forgive Jane, he was beginning to loathe Rossetti who he felt had betrayed his friendship. Once Morris had hero-worshipped Gabriel but now he was not far short of despising him, "It really is a farce our meeting when we can help it", he wrote to Aglaia on 25 November. He had first met Aglaia Coronio, the daughter of Alexander Ionides, in 1870 and they had developed a warm and, for Morris, somewhat flirtatious friendship. His feelings for her lacked the passion of those he felt for Georgie but in many ways this made Aglaia a more comfortable confidante and Morris's letters to her express, so far as he was able, the emotional confusion that he suffered during the 1870s.

Rossetti remained at Kelmscott Manor for the remainder of 1872 and the whole of 1873. But by 1874, Morris could no longer stand Rossetti's

left A WRITING TABLE IN THE TAPESTRY ROOM AT KELMSCOTT MANOR. THE BOOK IS COVERED WITH A MORRIS CHINTZ. IN 1889, MORRIS EXPERIMENTED WITH PRINTED LINEN COVERS BUT LATED ABANDONED THEM FOR VELLUM.

below MORRIS ASLEEP. A CARICATURE BY EDWARD BURNE-JONES.

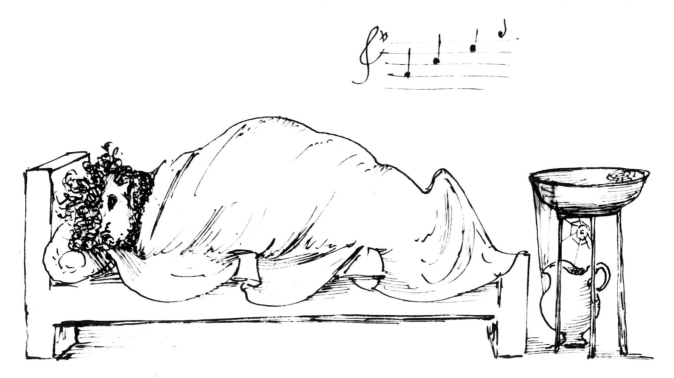

below ROSSETTI FIRST PAINTED JANE MORRIS AS *PROSERPINE*, THE TRAGICALLY IMPRISONED BRIDE OF PLUTO, IN 1872 AND WENT ON TO PAINT SEVEN FURTHER VERSIONS OF THIS HAUNTING AND POIGNANT IMAGE.

permanent occupation of the house they had agreed to share and wrote to Aglaia, "I feel that his presence there is a kind of slur on it: this is very unreasonable though when one thinks why we took the place, and how this year it really has answered that purpose." It was typical of Morris, schooled in self-sacrifice by his Anglo-Catholic mentor FB Guy, that he felt guilty about his perfectly reasonable resentment. In March he wrote to Aglaia again – "I am ashamed of myself for these strange waves of unreasonable passion: it seems so unmanly: yet indeed I have a good deal to bear considering how hopeful my earliest youth was, and what overwheening hopes I had of the joys of life." A month later he had steeled himself to confront Gabriel and wrote to him on 16 April saying that he had decided to relinquish his share of the lease "since you have fairly taken to living at Kelmscott, which I suppose neither of us thought you would do when we first began the joint possession of the house." Jane stayed at Kelmscott Manor for a week in June before departing for a holiday in Belgium with her husband, her daughters and the Burne-Jones's children Philip and Margaret. In a poignant letter to Aglaia written from the Hotel du Commerce in Bruges, William told her, "I am in the same room now as Janey and I were in when we came to Bruges on our wedding trip."

While the Morrises were abroad, Rossetti's friends removed him from Kelmscott after he had physically and verbally assaulted a group of innocent anglers in the belief that they were persecuting him. He returned to the closely-curtained house in Cheyne Walk suffering from paranoia; he was deluded and despairing.

On his return from Belgium, William Morris took out a further joint lease on the Manor with Frederick Startridge Ellis, his friend and publisher; so far as he was concerned, the serpent had been expelled from paradise. Jane's affair with Rossetti, she told her later lover Wilfrid Scawen Blunt, finished in 1875. Although he still adored her, his unpredictable behaviour frightened her and she felt powerless to lessen his addiction to drugs and whisky. She continued to sit for him until 1878 and remained his loving friend despite increasingly difficult circumstances, for the once ebullient and extrovert Gabriel was by then a haunted and suspicious recluse. He died at Birchington, on the Kent

coast, on 4 February 1882. "If you had known him you would have loved him", Jane told Blunt, "and he would have loved you – all were devoted to him who knew him. He was unlike all other men."

Rossetti's abrupt departure from Kelmscott Manor coincided with Morris's dissolution of The Firm. Although Warington Taylor had managed to avert the complete collapse of Morris, Marshall, Faulkner & Co. it was still barely profitable and Morris, seeing that only a radical shake-up would produce the required change, decided to buy out his partners and take sole control. The process was acrimonious and the negotiations prolonged, but Morris was determined and prepared to be ruthless and on 23 October the partnership was dissolved. Ford Madox Brown, who had contributed over 130 designs for stained glass during the previous 15 years, was the bitterest of the former friends, saying of Morris, "I could never meet him again with the least pleasure"; fortunately, the two were to be reconciled in 1886. Burne-Jones and Webb now had profitable careers of their own and were, in any case, to continue to design for Morris; Marshall and Faulkner had no objections. Rossetti, who had long since ceased to be an active participant, felt obliged to support his old friend and teacher Brown but, unlike Brown, did not need money. In an act at once cavalierly magnanimous and calculatedly cruel he asked that

above TILES OF ILLUSTRIOUS WOMEN, INCLUDING CLEOPATRA AND LUCRETIA, DESIGNED BY BURNE-JONES AND HAND-PAINTED FOR MORRIS, MARSHALL, FAULKNER & CO. IN THE EARLY 1860S.

overleaf THE FIREPLACE IN THE GREEN ROOM. THE BLUE AND WHITE TILES ARE "SWAN", DESIGNED BY WEBB BEFORE 1864, AND "ACANTHUS", A MORRIS DESIGN OF ABOUT 1870. THE ARMCHAIR IS COVERED IN THE "BIRD" FABRIC OF 1878.

his share of the compensation, £1,000, should be placed in a Trust for Janey; on 21 October Morris replied, "I have no objections to make."

From the Autumn of 1874 until his death 22 years later, Kelmscott Manor provided William Morris with a beloved retreat. There were times in London when he yearned for it and it never lost its magic or failed to give him ease and pleasure. Life there was simple and Morris relaxed. Even his relationship with the servants differed from that in London for they were countrymen, less dependent on his patronage than their city counterparts and unschooled in servility. Initially, the family was looked after by the Comely's and their daughter Annie, who lived in, and a village couple, the Judds, who lived out. It was Annie Comely, May recalled, who heroically saved the livestock from a sudden flood while wearing Morris's rubber Icelandic waders. Morris and the children enjoyed it when the swollen Thames broke its banks, inconvenience being outweighed by entertainment. The post was delivered by punt and the fat brown loaves of bread were thrown through the upper windows

left A TEA TABLE IN THE PANELLED ROOM. THE EBONIZED ARMCHAIR WAS DESIGNED BY ROSSETTI IN THE LATE 1860S AND WAS LATER MARKETED AS THE ROSSETTI CHAIR.

below THE MORRIS AND BURNE-JONES FAMILIES PHOTOGRAPHED AT THE GRANGE, FULHAM IN 1874. THE SPRIGHTLY GENTLEMAN STANDING TO MORRIS'S LEFT IS EDWARD'S FATHER.

by the baker's pitchfork. Morris, Jenny and May would take out the flat-bottomed boat and skim over the flooded meadows. In November 1875 he found himself stranded in the house and wrote to Jane – "I am rather short of victuals, as the booby Judd (female) only got me 1lb of bacon instead of 3 as I ordered her: however there will be enough I dare say... there is also one tin of kangaroo meat."

After the Comelys retired, Morris employed Mr and Mrs Giles, probably from 1887 when he wrote to May, who was in residence, asking her to hire a "house-keeping couple with children." In the 1880s and 1890s, Morris was acutely aware, as a Socialist, of the inequality between masters and servants but knew that any intimacy would be mutually embarrassing. As a busy man with an invalid and often absent wife it would have been impractical to employ no help and he also realized that in late Victorian capitalist society, domestic service served in part as a primitive form of social security. His self-consciousness is evident in his brusque directions to Sidney Cockerell, making his first visit in 1892, "At Lechlade my trap and man will meet you. Waggonette, brown horse, pepper and salt man NOT in livery."

Most of the guests at Kelmscott found the atmosphere relaxed, informal and industrious. The furnishings were both comfortable and practical rather than impressive and the walls were either whitewashed or hung with his own woven fabrics, a practical form of decoration in a house which must often have been damp. The wealthy and aristocratic Wilfrid Blunt, who stayed in 1889, found the house "romantic but extremely primitive." Three years later the ascetic George Bernard Shaw "is happy", according to Morris, "because (as he always sleeps with his window wide open) his water jug is frozen deeper than anyone else's."

Breakfast was usually served at 8.30am unless Morris had to return to London when a hurried departure was made at 6.30am to catch the 7.15am train from Lechlade to Paddington. The routine was familiar, work in the morning and leisure after lunch. Morris needed no weighty equipment for his work, he could write or design in his room at Kelmscott as easily as he could in his London study and guests could always help. Cockerell once found himself adding a coloured wash to the background of a textile design while Morris wrote and Jane sewed and Jenny knitted.

After dinner, where the talk was mainly of books and architecture, Morris would smoke a pipe with his male guests. He was a great pipe-smoker and anxious that his friends should share his pleasure, "Also bring a pipe with you: and if you don't like Latakia pure and simple, a little baccy as that is all I have down here", he wrote to George Howard in 1874. Latakia, a fine Turkish tobacco, was his favourite. When they rejoined the women they would play whist or word games, Twenty Questions was a particular favourite. Blunt recalled playing in 1894, "when the answers were the White Horse of White Horse Hill, Chaucer's pen and the American edition of Rossetti's *House of Life.*" In the later years, William and Janey usually played draughts or backgammon in the evening.

The river was Morris's particular joy and fishing his greatest pleasure. Ellis too was a keen angler and letters of the Kelmscott period are full of news of the latest catch; 22 gudgeon, a fine perch, an enormous pike, which were borne off to the kitchen for supper. He saw the river with the eyes of an artist and a naturalist and set out, as he had done as a boy in Epping Forest, to explore it inch by inch and to come to know and appreciate it in all weathers and seasons. "The river higher and the woods uncut...Altogether a very pleasant river to travel on, the bank being still very beautiful with flowers; the long purples and willow-herb, and that strong-coloured yellow flower very close and buttony are the great show: but there is a very pretty dark blue flower, I think mug-wort, mixed with all that besides the purple blossom of the horse-mint and mouse-ear and here and there a bit of meadow-sweet belated." This description, written to his daughter Jenny in the summer of 1888, is almost stream-of-consciousness, written as though in a boat on the flowing river with the sharp-eyed Morris describing what he sees as the banks speed by. Wild flowers, after all, inspired many of his designs.

The birds too, were a joy to him. "They were very beautiful about us", he wrote to Georgie, "I have been of late so steeped in London that it was quite a fresh pleasure to see the rooks about, who have been very busy in this showery weather. There was no lack of herons in these upper waters, and in the twilight the stint or summer snipe was crying about us and flitting from under the bank and across the stream: such a clean-made, neat-feathered, light grey little chap he is, with a wild musical little note, like all the moor-haunting birds." His love of Kelmscott suffuses his prose, he was comfortable there and comfortable with his friends. In August 1888, he expects a visit from Emery Walker and ends his note to him – "P.S. As everybody may be out when you come look under the mat and you will find the house key. Enter and be happy."

After Morris had dissolved The Firm and re-established it as Morris & Co. back in 1874, the necessity of increasing his income and his freedom from hampering partners resulted in a prolonged and prolific period of designing for wallpapers. Disregarding adaptations, Morris had created only six papers in the first 14 years of the firm but was to design

left MORRIS ASLEEP IN AN ARMCHAIR. A CARICATURE BY BURNE-JONES.

more than 30 between 1874 and 1895. Interior design was becoming fashionable among the growing middle classes and Morris's increased productivity was partly a response to a greater demand.

The sales of his papers must have been boosted by the publication in 1878 of *The Drawing Room* which recommended Morris products by name. It was written by Mrs Orrinsmith, the married name of Faulkner's sister Lucy, and sold over 6,000 copies in its first year.

More important to Morris, who somewhat surprisingly did not care much for wallpapers, were the printed cotton chintzes which he began to take an all absorbing interest in during 1875. The Firm had manufactured a small number of chintzes but it was not until Morris took sole control that printed textiles became an important and profitable line of merchandise. He spent the summer of 1875 in Leek at the factory of Thomas Wardle, George Wardle's brother-in-law, experimenting with natural dyes, particularly indigo blue, a dye he became intimately associated with as he spent a great part of the next few years with permanently stained blue forearms – "Your Old Prooshian Blue", as he signed letters to his beloved Jenny.

Jenny was the more academic of the Morris daughters, studious and bright and a great success at her school, but in the summer of 1876 when on holiday in Deal with her mother and sister she suffered an epileptic fit and by October she was having residential care in a weekly boarding school. Jenny's illness was the second great tragedy in Morris's life and, as in the first, he seems to have shouldered much of the blame perhaps assuming, although the idea was not generally held at the time, that the condition was hereditary. It is hard today to realize quite how appalling the diagnosis of epilepsy must have been to Jane and William Morris; in the 1870s little was known about the condition, epilepsy was not only an incurable illness but also an irredeemable stigma.

Morris reacted heroically; far from rejecting his daughter he loved her all the more. His letters to Jenny are designed to catch her interest, to amuse and entertain her, and involve her in his life and activities. They are careful, thoughtful, intelligent letters which combine mental stimulus and trivial gossip with reassuring love, ending with dozens of paper kisses. William Morris gave Jenny's needs all his attention, a quality sometimes absent in this busy, impatient and frankly self-opinionated man; she was to become tragically, as the condition worsened, the only fool he suffered gladly.

above ENTER MORRIS MOORED IN A PUNT, AND JACKS AND TENCHES EXEUNT. A CARICATURE BY DANTE GABRIEL ROSSETTI.

left MORRIS WAS A PASSIONATE ANGLER AND SPENT AS MUCH TIME AS POSSIBLE ON THE RIVER. THE RODS AND TACKLE LEAN AGAINST A MORRIS & CO. SETTLE DESIGNED BY WEBB.

above RUPES TOPSEIA, ROSSETTI'S
COMMENT, IN CARICATURE, ON
MORRIS'S DISSOLUTION OF THE FIRM
IN 1874. THE INCLUSION OF MARX
AND ENGELS SUGGESTS THAT IT DATES
FROM THE EARLY 1880S.

right THE SUMMERHOUSE AT
KELMSCOTT MANOR.

Janey's reaction was less constructive. Perhaps she too blamed Morris but it is more likely that the sheer enormity of what had happened to her daughter paralysed her emotions. She became nervous in Jenny's company and often insisted on separation. "Every time the thing occurs, it is as if a dagger were thrust into me", she told Blunt. Her genuine inability to cope with Jenny's illness placed extra emotional burdens on Morris, who had extra financial ones too (Jenny now needed professional care).

In 1873, the Morris's had left Queen Square (although William kept two rooms there), for Horrington House at Turnham Green in Chiswick. Morris wrote to Aglaia to tell her of the move adding, "It is a VERY little house with a pretty garden and I think will suit Janey and the children." Janey, banishing all thoughts of her own humble family home from her mind, described it as, "a very good house for one person to live in, or perhaps two." Morris seems to have liked the new house rather more than Jane. He was nearer the Burne-Jones family and every Sunday morning would walk over to Fulham for breakfast and a long chat with Ned in the studio. In 1875 they collaborated on a manuscript version of Virgil's *Aeneid*, Morris doing the calligraphy and illumination and Ned the illustrations – "It was to be wonderful, and put an end to printing", said Burne-Jones – but they were forced to abandon it after completing 177 pages. Ned's affair with Marie Zambaco was over and William's hopeless passion for Georgie had developed into a loving friendship. The two men were comfortable with each other again.

By 1877, Morris had tired of Horrington House and in November was trying, unsuccessfully, to let it together with the dragon of a housekeeper he employed. Jane and the children were on the Italian Riviera, wintering as the guests of George and Rosalind Howard at their villa in Oneglia. They were still there on 12 March 1878 when Morris wrote to Jane about The Retreat, a house he had inspected and was to name, to the confusion of succeeding generations, Kelmscott House.

KELMSCOTT HOUSE

*"Have nothing in your houses
which you do not know to be
useful or believe to be beautiful."*

WILLIAM MORRIS (1880)

THE PURCHASE OF 26 UPPER MALL, Hammersmith was not without elements of farce and once again Rossetti was the chief farceur. On 2 December 1877 he wrote to Jane Morris, convalescing in Oneglia, "I think I told you of Macdonald's house in Hammersmith Mall: favourable reports of it continue, and I am going myself to see it in a day or two." Rossetti was house-hunting, partly because the lease on Cheyne Row was up for renewal at an increased rental and partly because he was obsessed by the need for privacy and spent much time in the last few years of his life searching for his own Xanadu, "with walls and towers girdled round." By 19 December he had seen it and, as usual, found it wanting, reporting to Jane that the garden was over-looked and, the house subject to flooding, "Heaven knows where I can find rest for the sole of my foot."

Thus, when William Morris wrote to Jane on 12 March of the following year, she was already aware of the disadvantages of living on Hammersmith Mall. "I want to talk to you about the Macdonald's house...", he wrote to her in all innocence, "if you could be content to live no nearer London than that, I cannot help thinking we should do very well there...The house itself is just about big enough for us, and the rooms are mostly pretty – the drawing room is a great long room facing the river: the drawback to the house is a dreary room at the back: high, darkish and ugly-windowed: but we should only want it as a subsidiary 'larking room' – besides we might keep hens in it; or a pig, or a cow; or let it for a Ranter's Chapel."

Six days later he wrote again, having visited the house with Philip Webb. "The house could easily be done up at a cost of money, and might be made very beautiful with a touch of my art." Her fears about it being damp are groundless and she must have heard them from the Misses Cobden who had lodged next door and liked neither the house nor the Macdonalds. In an attempt to entice her, Morris writes, "we might perhaps manage to keep a pony and trap." On 28 March he sent her a full description of the accommodation and a plan of the garden and four days later Rossetti wrote with further misgivings, "The most serious blemish to the house is a frightful kitchen floor, perfectly dark and quite incommodious – the kitchen stairs being a sort of ladder with no lights at all, in which smashes would assail the ear whenever a meal was going on...Besides these objections, the place is very damp...I fear really it is not the place to suit the health of any of you."

By the time of Morris's next letter, on 2 April, he has arranged to take the house but in order to mollify Jane has had to agree to her suggestion that more staff will be needed, "We can easily house the 3rd maid & I think 'tis a good idea." Back in England at the end of May, Jane dismissed Rossetti's fears for her health, "We went to see the new house one day, of

previous page left SOCIALIST PAMPHLETS, WRITTEN BY MORRIS IN THE 1880S AND 1890S, REST ON A SUSSEX CHAIR IN THE COACH HOUSE AT KELMSCOTT HOUSE, THE MEETING ROOM OF THE HAMMERSMITH SOCIALISTS. THE MODERN HANGING IS "BLACKTHORN".

previous page right A STUDIO PORTRAIT OF MORRIS IN THE 1890S, PHOTOGRAPHED BY ELLIOTT AND FRY.

course much will have to be done before we go in, but really it does not seem damp after 6 or 7 months without fires; Webb says the overflow of Thames water can be prevented if proper means are taken." The pantomime was over.

Number 26 Upper Mall is a tall, imposing Georgian house built in the 1780s. Above the basement are three principal floors and three garret bedrooms lit by small dormer windows. Looking from the river, a two-story coach-house abuts the building to the left of the entrance front. Morris occupied the ground floor rooms, the one to the right of the central entrance hall being his bedroom and that to the left his study. The enormous and elegant drawing room which occupies the full width of the first floor, overlooking the river through five tall windows was, in theory at least, Jane's sitting room. Her bedroom, in an extension at the rear between the first and second floors, overlooked the garden. Jenny and May had two of the three second floor bedrooms and the attic rooms provided accommodation for the three maids; above the adjoining coach-house there were two further rooms.

The Macdonalds had converted the largest of the three basement kitchens into a dining room which may have served as the servants' hall

below THE DRAWING ROOM AT KELMSCOTT HOUSE. WEBB'S SETTLE FACES A "MORRIS" RECLINING CHAIR ACROSS THE FIREPLACE WHICH HOUSES WEBB'S GRATE, REMOVED FROM QUEEN SQUARE IN 1878.

after the Morrises moved in. Above this large, low-ceilinged room rose a magnificent dining room which retained its eighteenth-century plaster-work and mantelpiece and a huge, slightly-bowed, window with delicate glazing bars – this was the room that appeared to William to be dismal and "ugly windowed". Its classical proportions repelled him although even he had to confess that it was "handsome". To the medievally inclined Morris, with his love of asymmetry and romance, Georgian buildings seemed "Quite guiltless of picturesqueness, but are...solid and not inconvenient..They are at the worst not aggressively ugly or base, and it is possible to live in them without serious disturbance to our work or thoughts." Faint praise indeed, written in 1879, which bears out May's belief that he never "felt in his heart that the house he named Kelmscott House was our real home...No house in London could ever be invested with the passionate delight he had in our dear riverside home, the home of his dreams."

Morris took over the remaining lease of George Macdonald, a poet and writer, principally of children's books, who was vaguely known to him. Macdonald had lived there with his wife and many of their 11 children since 1867, and the house must have been distinctly crowded for he commandeered the huge drawing room as his study. According to Rossetti, Macdonald's study was "fearful to the eye" for he had commissioned a friend of his, an "artist" called Cottier, to decorate it. Cottier, of whom nothing seems to be known, covered the walls of the airy, light-filled room with crimson flock wallpaper, over which he stencilled fleur-de-lys in black paint, and painted the ceiling dark blue "with scattered stars in silver and gold, and a silver crescent moon." The house did indeed require a touch of Morris's art, but before he embarked on decoration his immediate preoccupation was to change the name of the house from The Retreat which he claimed sounded like a convent or at best a convalescent home – "People would think something was amiss with me and that your poor mama was trying to reclaim me", he wrote to May. He named it Kelmscott House, to the confusion of his friends, "Lord, my dear Janey," wrote Philip Webb in November, "What a magnificent title to the house at t'other end of the river – I must take care when I come to dinner, not to go off to Paddington to the other of that name."

William Morris was 44 years old when he moved into Kelmscott House and was already a man of note, "I am an artistic and literary man, pretty well known, I think, throughout Europe", he was to say in 1885 and it was already true. Although his latest book *Sigurd the Volsung*, written in both prose and verse, had proved too obscure for all but his most loyal admirers, his fame as a poet was ensured by *The Earthly Paradise* and he had only recently refused the Professorship of Poetry at Oxford, vacated by Tennyson. His business was prospering and his own productivity enormous. In 1877 he designed three new wallpapers and seven chintzes and maintained this level of creativity for virtually every year of the next decade. He had just opened a new show-room in Oxford Street which, although he disparaged it by saying "I can't say I am as much excited about it as I should be if it were a shed with half a dozen looms in it", must have been a source of justifiable pride. But Morris in 1878 was more than a bard and a businessman, for during the past two years he had involved himself for the first time in politics, the subject that was to dominate life at Kelmscott House. Morris's assault on the Victorian establishment, his "Crusade and Holy War against the age", was conducted on three fronts, Architectural, Political and Artistic, a Trinity which was for him inseparable.

In September 1876, while on his way to see his old Oxford friend Cormell Price at Broadway, he stopped in Burford where he was horrified by the restoration of the pretty medieval church. Victorian restoration was frequent and drastic, often involving near demolition, and the most notable Victorian restorer was the Gothic Revival architect Sir Gilbert Scott. It was not, in fact, Burford which provoked Morris to action, but Scott's proposed work on Tewkesbury Minster. On 10 March 1877, he wrote to *The Athenaeum*, "My eye just now caught the word 'restoration' in the morning paper, and on looking closer, I saw that this time it is nothing less than the Minster of Tewkesbury that is to be destroyed by Sir Gilbert Scott." Within weeks, The Society for the Protection of Ancient Buildings (SPAB) – Anti-scrape, as Morris called it – was founded with Morris as Secretary and Ruskin and Carlyle among the members. The latter joined because of a perceived threat to Sir Christopher Wren's City churches; William De Morgan recorded that Morris had to read out Carlyle's panegyric to Wren at the first public meeting – "Carlyle spoke of Wren's churches as 'marvellous works of art the like of which we shall never see again' – you may imagine Morris didn't relish it – and one heard it in the way he read it – I fancy he added mentally 'And a good job too'." For the remainder of his active life Morris was tireless in his work for the Society. He wrote to newspapers, corresponded acrimoniously with indignant clerics, visited and reported

above EDWARD BURNE-JONES AND WILLIAM MORRIS IN THE 1890s.

overleaf THE GARDEN AT KELMSCOTT HOUSE AS IT WAS IN THE EARLY TWENTIETH CENTURY. MORRIS WAS INTERESTED IN GARDEN DESIGN AND WROTE OF A TOWN GARDEN, "IT SHOULD BY NO MEANS IMITATE EITHER THE WILFULLNESS OR WILDNESS OF NATURE, BUT SHOULD LOOK LIKE A THING NEVER TO BE SEEN EXCEPT NEAR A HOUSE."

on buildings in peril and attended regular committee meetings which always ended with dinner, of chops or macaroni, at Gatti's in the Strand. The cause took more than Morris's time, it also cost him money, for after the founding of Anti-scrape, Morris & Co. refused to provide new windows for ancient buildings undergoing restoration; before 1877 over a third of their stained glass had been destined for such churches.

For Morris, the SPAB was a political movement, an attack on entrenched capitalism, as he made clear at the first Annual General Meeting in June 1878 when he said, "It is still only too commonly assumed that any considerations of Art must yield if they stand in the way of money interests." His views on art and design were equally anti-establishment, "I do not want art for the few, anymore than education for a few or freedom for a few", he told the Trades Guild of Learning when delivering his first lecture, "The Decorative Arts", in 1877.

His direct involvement in contemporary politics pre-dated Anti-scrape by a year. On 4 October 1876, he wrote a letter to *The Daily News* in support of William Gladstone's pamphlet, *The Bulgarian Horrors and the Question of the East*, published that September. Gladstone's pamphlet attacked the Conservative Government's support of the corrupt and vicious Ottoman Empire, a policy designed to contain Russian expansionism in the Balkans. Within weeks, Morris found himself the Treasurer of the Eastern Question Association, a largely Liberal movement opposed to armed intervention by Britain in the conflict between Russia and Turkey. By the end of the brief war, during which threats rather than action had protected British interests, the Liberal party had abandoned its principled opposition in the light of public Jingoism, and Morris, disillusioned by the experience, abandoned them. For the next five years he was a radical searching for a party in tune with his beliefs.

The decoration and furnishing of Kelmscott House reveals Morris's mature decorative style, an amalgam of elements taken from most of his previous houses handled with notable confidence. The massive pillared grate which Philip Webb had designed for Queen Square was now installed in the fireplace of the long first-floor drawing room. In the year they moved in, he designed "Bird", a double-woven woollen fabric which he now hung in folds around the room from floor to picture rail. These predominantly blue hangings were matched by a simple blue carpet which provided a neutral background for the subtle glowing colours of oriental rugs. Much of the furniture was of his own manufacture. A Webb settle, its high curved back painted with sunflowers, faced Burne-Jones's Chaucer wardrobe across the fireplace and "Morris" adjustable chairs provided more everyday comfort. The overmantel, above Webb's grate, supported large shimmering lustre plates made by Morris's friend William De Morgan and at the opposite end of the room sunken cupboards displayed opalescent ancient glass. Small Indian hexagonal tables, inlaid with ivory, stood among the chairs and a carved antique chest supported specimens of recently acquired Mughal brassware.

Morris's growing interest in the East was also evident in the high-ceilinged dining room which he had once found so dismal and drear. "Opposite the fireplace", May remembered, "stood the great Italian cypress-wood chest and thereon, with several pieces of oriental work, a pair of lordly peacocks of carved brass with jewelled necks, the guardians of a secret treasure. This side of the room had more than a touch of the Thousand and One Nights, for above this table of Eastern riches rose up a carpet spread like a canopy across the ceiling." "Eastern rugs were not to be trod on with hob-nailed boots", said Morris, and ensured that this magnificent late seventeenth-century carpet, the pride of his collection, received no such indignity. After his death, Janey sold it to the Victoria and Albert Museum, an appropriate home for he advised the Museum on Oriental textiles from 1880 until his death. The dining room was papered with his "Pimpernel" pattern and the wall which faced the window was fitted with a white painted dresser on which blue-and-white and pewter plates were displayed. The plain oak dining table, surrounded by antique carved oak chairs, was placed across the great bowed window. In this room paintings were allowed and Rossetti's portrait of *Mrs. William Morris in a blue silk dress* had pride of place above the Adam mantelpiece.

Rossetti's work also hung in Janey's bedroom, portrait drawings of her and of Jenny and May, posed for at Kelmscott Manor. Her quaint wooden jewel casket, painted for her by Gabriel and Lizzie Siddal as a wedding present, stood on a table near her bed. In 1883, Cobden-Sanderson, who she had encouraged to take up book-binding, bound a volume of Rossetti's poetry for her together with two volumes of Dante and a book "in Italian, printed on silk" which Gabriel had given her. Morris's ground floor rooms contained no such sentimental mementoes; according to May they "were almost frugally bare; in the study no carpets and no curtains; his writing table...a plain deal board and trestles, the walls nearly lined with books; just a fine inlaid Italian cabinet in one corner of the study." In photographs taken by

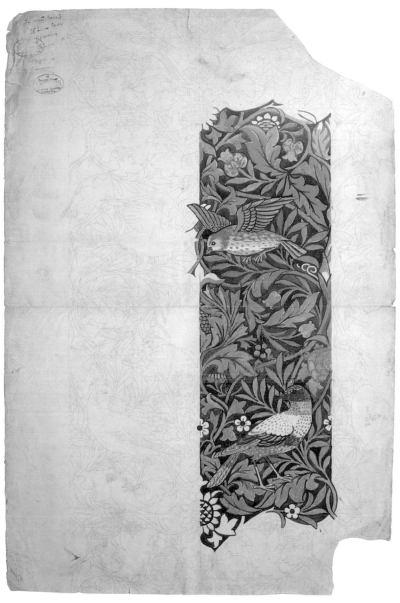

above MORRIS'S ORIGINAL DRAWING FOR "BIRD" DOUBLE-WOVEN FABRIC, DESIGNED IN 1878 FOR THE DRAWING ROOM OF KELMSCOTT HOUSE.

Emery Walker in the 1890s, the study is papered with "Trellis" and ebonized rush-seated Sussex chairs are clearly visible. On his work table, May tells us, among the papers, quills, books, pipes and tobacco-jar of Latakia, there was usually an intricately carved or embossed small box or two which he loved to fondle, rather like worry beads. In addition, there was perhaps also a small flask of rose or lavender-water with which he would dab his large bandanna handkerchief.

Morris's study was no ivory tower. "Indeed the very position...hard on the road within sound of screaming children from the slum, of the postman's knock and the milkman's yell, of all the coming and going of visitors past his door, a room no whit retired from the daily movement of the house, this is itself typical of the ordering of his life", wrote May. His ability to work under trying circumstances was also noted by Blunt

above MORRIS'S HAMMERSMITH STUDY WITH "TRELLIS" PAPER ON THE WALLS. ONE OF HIS FINE COLLECTION OF MEDIEVAL MANUSCRIPTS IS DISPLAYED ON THE WORK TABLE.

left ONE OF MORRIS'S MANY PIPES. ACCORDING TO AN INTERVIEW FOR *THE WOMAN'S SIGNAL* IN 1894, HE WAS TONGUE-TIED WITHOUT TOBACCO.

during a visit to Kelmscott Manor. "He worked at the designs he was making for his carpets, and at his drawings, and the corrections of his proofs in a room where he was liable every minute to disturbance...it was this insensitiveness to his surroundings that enabled him to deal with the prodigious volume of work which he daily assigned himself, both manual and intellectual."

During the late 1870s, when Kelmscott was being decorated, Morris was formulating his principles of interior design for his lectures and trying to reconcile his innate love of the finest, and therefore most expensive, materials and techniques with his growing awareness that his products were only affordable by the rich. "Simplicity" was his new keynote – "Simplicity of life, even the barest, is not a misery, but the very foundation of refinement", but "this simplicity you may make as costly as you please or can", he wrote in 1880 in his lecture "The Beauty of Life", ending his paragraph with the famous dictum, "Have nothing in your houses which you do not know to be useful or believe to be beautiful."

William Morris was one of those individuals whose activities expand to fill the space available and it soon became clear that Janey was not to have her pony and trap. By the end of the year, Hammersmith rugs were being hand-knotted by nimble-fingered women in the coach-house. Now that his experiments in dyeing were reaching a satisfactory conclusion, Morris's principal interest was weaving, in all its aspects. In 1879, he began to weave his first tapestry, working on a loom that he had installed in his bedroom. For 516 hours, "Acanthus and Vine", or "Cabbage and Vine" as Morris self-deprecatingly named it, was worked on during snatched early morning moments between 10 May and 17 September. But it was not completed until two years later. Morris believed tapestry to be the highest of all art forms and was determined to rescue it from the dire condition into which it had sunk, and elevate it to its true medieval glory. Satisfied by his own experiment that it could be done he imported looms and a weaver from France and installed them in Queen Square.

Fortunately for his family, whose home was rapidly becoming a branch of Morris & Co., he was looking for new premises. The manufacture of many of the firm's products was carried out by outside contractors which occasionally led to problems over quality and he wished, where possible, to reduce his dependence on others and increase the manufacturing potential of his own company. After a lengthy and frustrating search, De Morgan finally found suitable buildings on the bank of the river Wandle at Merton. In June 1881, Morris acquired the lease of a former cotton printing works housed in a number of picturesque but ramshackle weather-boarded buildings in the grounds of the long demolished medieval Merton Abbey. The weaving, dyeing, printing and stained glass departments of Morris & Co. moved to Merton from the

left A WEBB-TILED FIREPLACE AT KELMSCOTT HOUSE. MORRIS WAS HIGHLY CRITICAL OF LATE VICTORIAN FIREPLACES. "TRUMPERY OF CAST-IRON, AND BRASS AND POLISHED STEEL AND WHAT NOT – OFFENSIVE TO LOOK AT, AND A NUISANCE TO CLEAN."

cramped and unsuitable premises in Queen Square and with them went the coach-house carpet looms.

Merton Abbey soon became far more than a works for both his employees and his family. The former were well cared for and paid above average wages. The teenage boys who worked on the tapestry looms slept in a dormitory during the week and were looked after by a house-keeper; in order to encourage their self-education he provided a circulating library. Morris also kept simple accommodation for himself, just as he had done at Queen Square. The works at Merton were set in seven acres which included a meadow for drying the freshly dyed cottons after they had been rinsed in the river, an orchard and a vegetable garden; a pool was stocked with perch transferred from Kelmscott Manor. Morris delighted in the garden and the fruit trees, and the happy mixture of wild and cultivated flowers. "I was at Merton yesterday", he wrote in March 1884, "A beautiful spring day and the garden covered with primroses and violets; the daffodils in huge quantities almost out, and a beautiful almond tree in blossom relieved against our black sheds looking lovely."

The journey from Hammersmith to Merton was not an easy one and involved him going on the Underground (which he detested), travelling from Hammersmith to Faringdon Street, walking across the City to Ludgate Hill and taking a train to Merton, a journey of two hours. On occasion he preferred to walk, "On Tuesday and on Thursday I walked all the way to Merton by Roehampton Lane: really a pleasant walk: I am quite sick of the Underground, and think I shall often walk to or from Merton. It takes a long two hours; but you see it is not all pure waste like the sweltering train-business. I came back in an open trap on Tuesday", he wrote to Jenny in 1883. Friends visited him at the works, leaving "laden with marsh-marigolds, wallflowers, lilac & hawthorn", and May remembered that a day at Merton was an outing for the family. From 1883, Morris employed his unsuccessful brother Edgar at Merton; he was seen there by Blunt in 1892: "I was at Merton with the Morrises, when we saw a brother of his, working in the dye vats there, a dreamy man in workman's clothes, with his shirt sleeves turned up, and his arms blue with indigo to the elbows."

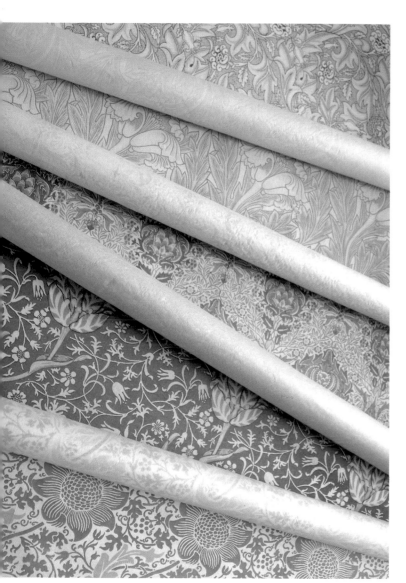

above MORRIS CHINTZES AT KELMSCOTT HOUSE. FROM TOP TO BOTTOM: "LEA", 1885; "TULIP", 1875; "POMEGRANATE", 1877; "MEDWAY", 1885, AND "KENNET", 1883.

right "STRAWBERRY THIEF", A PRINTED COTTON THAT WAS DESIGNED BY MORRIS IN 1883.

AN EXCURSION

Despite his increasing responsibilities in the 1880s, Morris still loved fun. "Wot larx!" he would write to Jenny, and in 1880 he arranged an expedition, made possible by the felicitous siting of his London and country homes, to travel between them by boat. The news that Janey was to join the party astonished Christina Rossetti who wrote to her brother in August, "I might also gasp a moment at the vision of beautiful Mrs. Morris with her family boating on the river Thames for a week; not only (I trust) with a cabin, but, I surmise, needing one." Apart from William and Jane, the adventurous party included Jenny and May and their friend Elizabeth Macleod, Crom Price, William De Morgan and the Hon. Richard Grosvenor a friend of the latter and a member of Antiscrape; Eliza, a housemaid, travelled some of the way. Fortunately, Morris kept a humorous log of the voyage which he circulated later for comments by the other participants and thus their amusements and mishaps are recorded in some detail.

The day of their departure on 10 August was a beautiful summer's day and Morris was beside himself with anticipatory pleasure – "Little things please little minds", he wrote to Georgie Burne-Jones before they set off, "therefore my mind must be little, so pleased am I this morning." He and Jenny had rushed out before breakfast to see the craft on which they were to travel – the *Ark*, hired from Salter of Oxford, which must have sailed in during the night and moored below Morris's water-gate.

The *Ark* was accompanied by the *Albert*, a rowing boat hired from Biggens who had also, presumably, delivered the vessels as two of their men were on hand to row the *Ark* to Kew. The party finally embarked at 3pm having delayed to catch the tide; Morris and Crom Price rowed the *Albert*. At Kew, the boats were attached to a string of barges and towed "by a mercantile tea-kettle" to Twickenham where rowing re-commenced. Biggens' men were dismissed at Teddington Lock and the *Ark* was towed by a man with a horse to Kingston where he was replaced by a man with a pony, sent from Oxford, who was to remain with them for the rest of the journey. They finally reached their destination, The Magpie Inn at Sunbury, at 10.15pm in darkness.

On the Wednesday, they reached Windsor Bridge at sunset, "beautiful and very hazy", after an uneventful day punctuated by Morris's oaths as he barked his shins or grazed his knuckles – "(Note by author", he wrote in the log, "this narrative may and should be filled up at frequent intervals with such expletives as may seem to fit the occasion without fear of corrupting the text in any way leaning towards exaggeration of the facts)". Then, in the early evening of the next day they were towed, like

"She is odd but delightful: imagine a biggish company boat with a small omnibus on board, fitted up luxuriously inside with two shelves and a glass-rack, and a sort of boot behind this: room for two rowers in front, and I must say for not many more."

MORRIS ON THE *ARK*

an extremely slow bull in a china shop, into the middle of Maidenhead Regatta – "The Ark was sculled majestically through a crowd of inferior craft and passed under Maidenhead Bridge not without dignity amidst considerable excitement", wrote Morris, facetiously, in the log. To Georgie he confessed, "you may think we were chaffed a little." The inelegant and cumbersome boat steered by the stout, blue-clad Morris on the roof, the medieval Jane sewing while reclining on cushions, and the bald, flushed De Morgan straining at the oars must indeed have delighted the spectators who, several deep, lined both banks of the river.

On the Friday they ran aground at Wargrave – "All the males of the party gave conflicting orders in loud tones (mostly emphatic); eventually De Morgan restored order and happiness by taking off his boots and socks, stepping into the mud and pushing her off." That night they all dined at The White Hart at Sonning where they had an excellent supper, Morris bent a knife in two while arguing with Price and a lady howled songs overhead.

The next night they reached Wallingford where they "took up quarters at The Town Arms Hotel kept by one Thirza Ransom; place smelt horrible." They woke to an overcast grey sky and decided that Wallingford was a "dirty looking, uncomfortable town." Their tempers were not improved by "abominable extortion in the charges of Thirza Ransom", but they revenged themselves by warning "all the people on both banks of the river to avoid The Town Arms Hotel." They lunched above Clifton lock where Morris, "(though angry) was appointed cook with excellent results as on two former occasions." By 8.30pm they had reached Oxford and the *Ark* was safely moored in Salter's Boatyard. They stayed the night at The King's Arms and on the following morning Jane Morris departed for Kelmscott Manor by train and the rest continued by river in two rowing boats towed by William Bossom and his man, the same Bossom who had supplied Morris with a flat-bottomed boat to navigate the river Seine in the year before his marriage.

They travelled slowly on this last stage of the journey home for the river was increasingly narrow and on occasion the boats had to be manhandled around hazards on rollers. Morris caught a perch at New Bridge, "called so because it was built in the fourteenth century and remains untouched to this day". Bossom and his man then returned to Oxford and they picnicked on large quantities of ham and sardines, bread, cheese, champagne and soda-water. They arrived at Kelmscott in darkness at 10.30pm, their course illuminated by a single candle in the prow of the leading boat. "Charles was waiting for us with a lantern at our bridge by the corner...and presently the ancient house had me in its arms again: Janey had lighted it all brilliantly, and sweet it all looked, you may be sure."

"A noteworthy feature of this journey was, that everybody perpetually gave orders in a very loud voice, & that nobody ever paid the slightest attention to them."

JENNY'S COMMENT IN
THE LOG BOOK

overleaf A FISHING PICNIC BY THE THAMES. MORRIS LOVED AL FRESCO MEALS AND WAS DEEPLY DISTRESSED ON ONE OCCASION WHEN BURNE-JONES HID THE ROAST FOWL THEY HAD TAKEN AND CONVINCED MORRIS THAT THEY HAD FORGOTTEN TO BRING IT.

"THE EARTHLY PARADOX"

CAPTION TO A CARTOON OF 1886

above THE MEMBERSHIP CARD OF THE DEMOCRATIC FEDERATION DESIGNED BY MORRIS IN 1883.

On 13 January 1883, William Morris received an honourary Fellowship from Exeter College, Oxford, and on the same day he joined the Democratic Federation, a socialist organization recently founded by Henry Mayers Hyndman, a wealthy, autocratic, renegade Tory. The two events neatly symbolize Morris's life in the 1880s: on the one hand he was a member by birth and distinction of the Victorian Establishment, on the other he was out to destroy it. In 1880, he decorated Rounton Grange for Sir Lothian Bell, a wealthy iron-founder, while complaining to his amazed client that he hated ministering to "the swinish luxury of the rich". In the very same year, his Company was re-furbishing the Throne Room at St James's Palace, the epicentre of the British class system presided over by Queen Victoria, the hated "Empress Brown" to use the soubriquet coined by De Morgan, which implied a scandalous relationship between the Monarch and her faithful ghillie John Brown. In 1882, Morris read Karl Marx's *Das Kapital* in French as there was no English translation, and two years later had it exquisitely and expensively bound by TJ Cobden-Sanderson in dark blue leather with elaborate gold tooling. Morris was the first "champagne socialist", a criticism he was well aware of and found hard to refute. He eventually adopted the position that until the radical changes in society that he hoped for came about, it would hardly be fair to sacrifice his family and employees to salve his own conscience, a perfectly reasonable position.

When Morris joined the Democratic Federation – which added the prefix Social to its title a year later – he took Philip Webb and Charles Faulkner with him, but not Edward Burne-Jones. The latter could neither understand Morris's politics nor abide his constant talk about them. As a result, their friendship almost foundered and the Sunday morning breakfasts ceased in April 1884. Morris's move to the revolutionary left was seen as extreme by many of his friends. Tennyson told Allingham, "He has gone crazy", and Morris took care to keep news of his political activities from his elderly mother. Janey seems to have stood aloof from her husband's socialism but, unlike Georgie, does not appear to have been sympathetic. Jenny was too often ill to participate, but May followed her father whole-heartedly. After his death, Morris's political beliefs were played down by Mackail and virtually treated as a temporary aberration but, in fact, they dominated his life between the early 1880s and the early 1890s. He gave the movement his time, his money, his intellect and his creativity and, some would say, his health.

The early organization of the Labour movement in Britain is complex and subject to dissentions, splits, re-groupings and schisms, as Morris's personal socialist career bears out. However, he was remarkably consistent in his views, which were arrived at empirically. He looked at society and perceived inequality which he thought wrong and determined to do his best to improve things. His one rule, he said, "in looking into matters social and political", was "that in thinking of the condition of any body of men I should ask myself 'How could you bear it yourself?'" By reading *Das Kapital*, Morris found an intellectual and economic structure for his own ideas – revolution he felt, and now knew, was inevitable. Morris was not a liberal socialist, he was a red-blooded communist agitator; class-war was his aim even though he knew that he might find himself among the plutocrats facing the proletarian firing-squads. He did not believe that the workers should be led by middle-class intellectuals like himself but saw his role as an educational one; he felt that the working classes must be awakened from apathy in order to organize the re-formation of society themselves.

Throughout his political years, his arguments with his comrades revolved around two major issues; "gradualism" and individual freedom. Gradualism, the policy adopted by the Fabian Society among

others, was intended to change society by democratic means by encouraging the election of Socialist candidates to the House of Commons. Morris was strongly opposed to this as he believed, quite correctly, that by doing so the socialists would be absorbed effortlessly into the capitalist system. Minor adjustments would be made, extension of the franchise for instance, or the amelioration of working conditions, but society would still be ruled by the profit motive. Radical change could only be brought about by bloody revolution.

Individual freedom in a post-revolutionary society posed other problems. He was against State-Socialism, the system that was to prevail in Eastern Europe for much of the twentieth century, which, he foresaw, could result in a tyranny as oppressive as any devised by the capitalists. At the same time he could see that individual freedom which was totally uncontrolled by society resulted in anarchy which he found impractical and divisive. The nearest he came to a solution may be found in *News from Nowhere*, the Utopian socialist novel he wrote in 1889/90, in which democracy functions at village pump level and decisions are reached by reasoned argument and common consent.

For the moment, in 1883, he was involved in the practicalities of the movement. Shortly after joining the Social Democratic Federation he was elected Treasurer and was also editing, subsidizing and distributing its magazine, *Justice*. Old friends were cajoled into helping: a surprised Swinburne, the ex-high priest of decadence, was told by Morris, "You ought to write us a song, you know, that's what you ought to do: I mean to be set to music, for singing at meetings of the faithful." His energy for the cause was astonishing – during two weeks in 1884 he lectured in London, Hampstead, Blackheath, Manchester, Ancoats and Leicester, while running a large business for which he was also the chief designer and caring for an ill wife and an iller daughter. Over the next five years he averaged six or seven lectures a month in addition to open-air meetings, demonstrations and endless committee meetings. In 1885, he made the first of his annual visits to Scotland which were to continue until 1889. He was in a constant rush, as he told Jenny – "with all this lateness we were too hurried to stop anywhere for grub, all I could do at Carlisle was to rush to the buffet and catch up whatever came first to hand 2 mutton pies as it happened but I was very hungry and they were very good. Tell your mother I am none the worse for them today."

In December 1884, Morris resigned from the Federation over the question of gradualism and took with him the majority of the executive, including Eleanor Marx and Belfort Bax, to form the Socialist League which held its meetings in Morris's coach-house, just as the Hammersmith branch of the Social Democratic Federation had done.

On 1 September 1885, he was arrested following a Free Speech demonstration and charged with assaulting a policeman. The charge was dismissed by a bemused magistrate and the popular press had a field day. *The Earthly Paradox* was a typical comment, a cartoon showing a weeping policeman cleaning Morris's boots; in the England of the mid-1880s false arrest and police brutality were reserved for the working classes. Nevertheless there was justifiable fear of the police who were consistently antagonistic to the socialists. On 13 November 1887, during an illegal occupation of Trafalgar Square, aggressive police action resulted in the death of Alfred Linnell, a young married man. His funeral cortege on 16 December was the largest in London since that of the Duke of Wellington and Morris wrote a *Death Song* which was sold for the benefit of his widow and orphans.

Morris devoted his literary talents to the cause (although being Morris he did find the time to publish a verse translation of Homer's *Odyssey* in 1887) and edited *Commonweal*, the newspaper of the Socialist League, from 1884 to 1890. In its pages he wrote and published not only editorials and journalism but also his two great optimistic socialist fables, *A Dream of John Ball* and *News from Nowhere*.

above MEMBERS OF THE HAMMERSMITH SOCIALIST SOCIETY PHOTOGRAPHED BY EMERY WALKER IN THE GARDEN OF KELMSCOTT HOUSE IN 1890/91. MORRIS IS SEATED IN THE FRONT ROW NEXT TO MRS MAUGHAM WHO WEARS A STRIPED SKIRT.

The Sunday evening meetings of the Hammersmith branch of the Socialist League were lively affairs for Morris's fame and connections attracted notable speakers and large audiences. When he was not lecturing, Morris usually took the chair where he spent much of his time doodling or indulging in fits of the "fidgetts". Bernard Shaw who was a frequent speaker described his first visit to a meeting of the League – "Here then was Morris in his blue suit and bluer shirt, his tossing mane which suggested that his objection to looking-glasses extended to brushes and combs, and his habit, when annoyed by some foolish speaker, of pulling single hairs violently from his moustache and growling 'Damned fool!'" His increasing dogmatism was noted by many of his friends including Blunt and James Wilkes, a member of the League, who recorded Morris's habit of prefacing his opinions with the phrase "in point of fact" – "In point of fact", said Morris, "Wordsworth was an ass."

After the meeting, the principal speaker and other chosen guests were invited into the house for supper. In 1888, the working-class Scottish comrade Bruce Glasier found that, "The dining room lit up with large

William Morris
speaking from
a wagon in Hyde
Park May 1 1894

above A SKETCH BY WALTER CRANE OF
MORRIS WEARING HIS SOFT FELT HAT
AND BLUE SERGE SUIT, ADDRESSING A
SOCIALIST RALLY IN 1894.

candles on brass or copper candlesticks...was magnificently grand." Jane was there on this occasion although she was often absent, spending most winters in Italy with the Howards and much of the summer at Kelmscott Manor or south coast resorts. Janey's only recorded witticism was made at one of these Sunday evening meals, at the expense of Bernard Shaw. "When I presently found myself dining at Kelmscott House my position was positively painful; for the Morris meals were works of art almost as much as the furniture. To refuse Morris's wine or Mrs. Morris's viands was like walking on the great carpet with muddy boots...I am a vegetarian and teetotaller. Morris did not demur to the vegetarianism: he maintained that a hunk of bread and an onion was a meal for any man; but he insisted on a bottle of wine to wash it down. Mrs. Morris did not care whether I drank wine or water; but abstinence from meat she regarded as a suicidal fad. Between host and hostess I was cornered; and Mrs. Morris did not conceal her contempt for my folly. At last pudding time came; and as the pudding was a particularly nice one, my abstinence vanished and I showed signs of a healthy appetite. Mrs. Morris pressed a second helping on me, which I consumed to her entire satisfaction. Then she said 'That will do you good: there is suet in it.' and that is the only remark, as far as I can remember, that was ever addressed to me by this beautiful, stately and silent woman."

May, who was musical, was in charge of the Socialist League choir and conducted them when they sang the *Chants for Socialists* which her father had written in 1884. In 1883 he bought her a guitar from Magnusson, for £6.10s, and when Janey acquired a mandolin two years later they would play duets together. Morris, whose musical tastes were primitive, quite liked the sound of stringed instruments but hated the piano which could not be practised when he was in the house. His mother had bought them one as a family Christmas present in 1879 and his thank-you letter was polite rather than enthusiastic - "I have to thank you so very much, dearest mother, for your splendid gift of the piano: I shall be calling at Broadwood's tomorrow and will hear about it", wrote Morris, gritting his teeth. Oddly enough he affected a love of bagpipe music – "Like an amiable small pig squealing you know."

Jane was always absent for Morris's annual boat-race party, an event that was virtually *de rigueur* if you lived by the river. The first seems to

left MAY MORRIS WITH HER GUITAR.
SHE WAS AN ENTHUSIASTIC AND
ACCOMPLISHED PLAYER.

have been held in 1882 when he invited George Howard whose wife Rosalind was prominent in the Temperance movement. "Do any of your party care to come to the boatrace on Saturday? They shall be very welcome and shall not be COMPELLED to drink anything save water." Three years later he wrote to May, in Italy with her mother, "These boatrace parties are funny things: there were several strangers (Miss B's friends) and the Avelings; also Master Poole: of course the people one would have liked to make merry with went early and the strangers stayed late." It may have been this party, when Morris was decidedly grumpy, that Violet Hunt attended – "Once, after a truly good lunch at Kelmscott House, from whose...wide windows we had surveyed the boat

race, he met us all trooping out of the dining room and greeted us severally with – 'Well, are you full?'" In 1887, he decided to solve the problem of unwelcome guests by issuing formal invitations, "Because you know my dear", he wrote to Jenny, "if we don't, all sorts of disagreeable people are to be asked." But even then there was bad behaviour, "A good many of them would go on the roof, and sit outside of it: Bah! It makes me giddy to think of it – and O how black their hands were afterwards." In 1892 the workers from Merton Abbey were invited – "The boat-race is over and so is my entertainment. Annie provided splendidly for us: The men I think were a little shy, but I think they enjoyed themselves: the day was most brilliant. Oxford won the race; but I suppose you care for that as little as I do", he told Jenny.

Early in 1890, when the final instalment of *News from Nowhere* had appeared, Morris was ousted from the editorship of *Commonweal* and he resigned from the Socialist League. The League had been subject to internal divisions for some time and by now the Anarchist faction was in the ascendent and Morris had had enough. With his departure went his money, for he had regularly subsidized the League's activities, and within months it was in disarray. He reconstituted the Hammersmith branch, most of whose members had remained loyal, as the Hammersmith Socialist Society and the weekly meetings continued as before. But Morris lived to see gradualism prevail. Independent Labour Party candidates won seats in the General Election of 1892, and although he remained a committed Socialist until his dying day his own position became more peripheral and he was content to let others continue the work which he had begun. His fierce commitment of the 1880s was over, his heart was no longer in the movement to which he had devoted so much concentrated work and energy.

In February 1891, Morris became severely ill with both gout and an infected kidney. According to Mackail, his doctors told him that, "Henceforth he must consider himself an invalid to the extent of husbanding his strength and living under a very careful regime." He had suffered from debilitating attacks of gout since his twenties and as he grew older their severity increased. In 1878, when he had gone to join Jane in Italy shortly after acquiring the lease of Kelmscott House, he had fainted from the pain in Genoa and was crippled throughout their visit to Venice. In 1885 he was housebound for over a month in October and early November and, to his great annoyance, had to be wheeled from his bed to a couch in his study. "The difficulty is that I can't get a shoe on yet and I don't know how to get from the carriage to the house if it is wet", he told Jenny. From 1891, the hectic travelling had to stop and the Sunday morning sessions on his soap box at the base of Hammersmith Bridge, in his "loose blue serge suit and soft felt hat", were largely over.

right THE FRONTISPIECE OF THE KELMSCOTT PRESS EDITION OF *NEWS FROM NOWHERE*, 1892, BY CHARLES MARCH GERE, SHOWING THE ENTRANCE ON THE EAST SIDE OF KELMSCOTT MANOR.

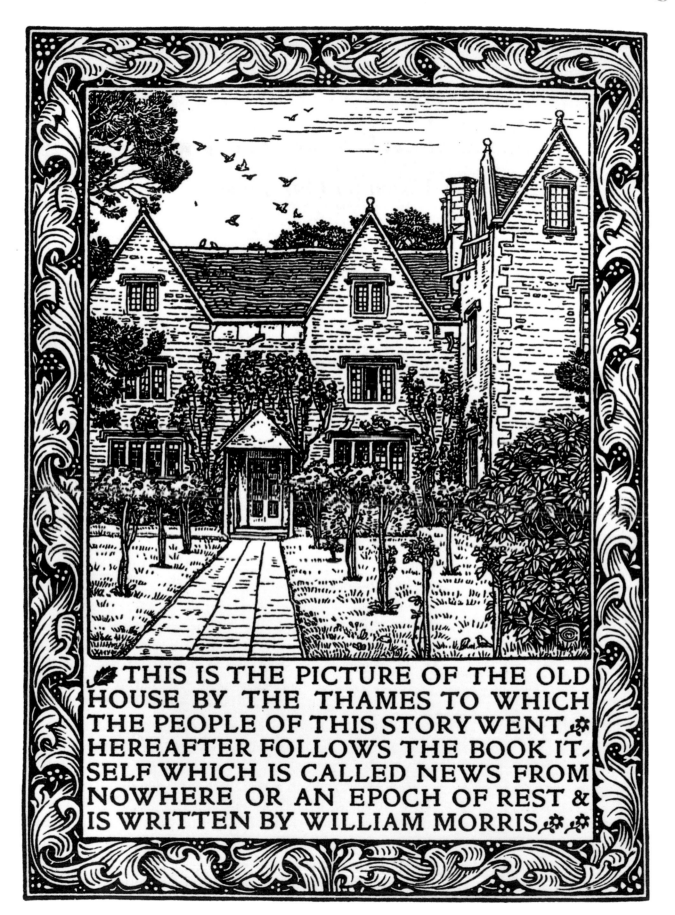

THIS IS THE PICTURE OF THE OLD HOUSE BY THE THAMES TO WHICH THE PEOPLE OF THIS STORY WENT. HEREAFTER FOLLOWS THE BOOK IT. SELF WHICH IS CALLED NEWS FROM NOWHERE OR AN EPOCH OF REST & IS WRITTEN BY WILLIAM MORRIS.

Illness and worry seemed to surround him during these years; his beloved Charlie Faulkner who had been severely paralysed by a stroke since the October of 1888 died early in 1892, Jane had suffered a prolonged period of illness in the late 1880s and Jenny's condition was a permanent source of anxiety. May's marriage to Henry Halliday Sparling on 10 June 1891 caused both her parents great concern. Sparling was an educated but ineffectual young socialist for whom Morris had found employment and May married him in the aftermath of an unsatisfactory liaison with Bernard Shaw. They were right to be worried for the marriage foundered, largely through Shaw's mischievous intervention, and the two separated four years later. Morris was still ill in July, recuperating in Folkestone, when he decided to take Jenny to France for a holiday. They were away for a fortnight, touring the familiar northern towns. In Abbeville they bought Janey a present, "in the form of a wide-mouthed jug with comic lady and gentleman on it, rude, modern, but traditional pottery", he wrote to her, "Jenny would have it for you – don't fear it only cost 3F.50."

Jane had no reason to worry about this rash expenditure for the year before, in March 1890, Morris had relinquished sole control of Morris & Co. and entered into a partnership with the Company's joint commercial managers Robert and Frank Smith. In retrospect, it almost seems as though he had a premonition of his illness for by taking on partners he was able to share the burden of his business and also ensure a substantial income for himself and his family for the foreseeable future. The terms of the partnership, which were extremely generous to the Smiths, allowed Morris to gradually reduce his investment to 50% of the capitalized value while the Smiths increased theirs to 25% each. Morris was to draw his share of the profits and £1,000 of his capital annually which gave him an income of over £5,000 a year during the 1890s and the freedom to write and follow his interests for the remainder of his life.

Morris's decision may well have been influenced by a new and all-consuming passion which he realized would require a capital outlay; the printing of beautiful books. In 1888 he had joined The Art Workers' Guild, an organization of artist-craftsmen which owed much of its existence to his own example, and on 15 November he attended a lecture on printing given by his Hammersmith neighbour and fellow socialist Emery Walker. As they walked home together Morris told Walker of his desire to set up a Private Press and Walker, who was an expert process-engraver, must have told him of the practical difficulties. By 1890, Morris had decided to embark on "a little typographical adventure."

"If I were asked to say what is at once the most important production of Art and the thing most to be longed for, I should answer, A beautiful House", said Morris, "And if I were further asked to name the production next in importance and the thing next to be longed for, I should answer, A beautiful Book." His interest in beautiful books was no new passion and dated at least from the days of *The Big Picture Book* of the mid-1860s. Between hearing Walker's lecture and setting up his press Morris had taken a close interest in the printing of his most recent fiction, the archaic *House of the Wolfings*, of 1889, and *The Roots of the Mountains* of 1890, both of which were printed at the Chiswick Press. In the early months of 1891 he asked them to print several proof pages of his new work, *Gunnlaug's Saga* in a replica of one of William Caxton's fifteenth-century types but agreed that the experiment was unsuccessful. There was nothing for it but to design his own fonts and print them at his own Press which, like his London house was to be named Kelmscott after his beloved Manor.

"It was the essence of my undertaking to produce books which it would be a pleasure to look upon as pieces of printing and arrangement of type", he wrote in 1895, and it is a revealing statement for it is written from the point of a bibliophile rather than that of a reader. Morris had collected fifteenth-century printed books since the mid-1860s when he first met the antiquarian bookseller FS Ellis who was to become his publisher and friend. But in 1880 he sold much of his library and made further sales throughout that decade to help finance his political activities. In the late 1880s he began to buy again and eventually amassed over 800 early printed books including over 100 fifteenth-century German wood-

left THE OXFORD AND CAMBRIDGE BOAT RACE PASSING KELMSCOTT HOUSE IN 1892. MORRIS'S GUESTS THAT YEAR WERE HIS WORKMEN FROM MERTON ABBEY.

cut books and examples of fine French, Italian, Dutch and Spanish printing. He excused his extravagance by claiming that they were the tools of
his trade but he could hardly say the same of the illuminated manuscripts that he also acquired. In fact, he was in love with them with the
same depth of emotion which he normally reserved for ancient buildings
or the English countryside, he loved the feel and the smell of them and
their antiquity. Many of the books were bought from the leading dealer
Bernard Quaritch and some idea of the scale of his purchasing may be
seen in their accounts of 1892 when Quaritch owed the Kelmscott Press
£1,350 for books received for sale and Morris owed Quaritch £1,237.7s.5d
for the purchase of books and manuscripts.

It was Morris's intention that the books printed by the Kelmscott Press would rival those of the great fifteenth-century printers so dear to him and it was therefore necessary that their techniques and materials should be similar. "It was a matter of course that I should consider it necessary that the paper should be hand made, both for the sake of durability and appearance", he wrote, and sure enough on 22 October 1890, Morris and Walker visited the paper mill of Joseph Batchelor in Kent taking a fifteenth-century book as an example. By January 1891 Morris had rented premises at 14 and 16 Upper Mall, hard by Kelmscott House, hired a retired Master Printer, William Bowden, and his daughter Mrs Pine and designed his first typeface "Golden", a 14-point Roman font based on fifteenth-century Venetian print.

The first book issued by the Press was his own *Story of the Glittering Plain*, which was completed by early May when Blunt was visiting Kelmscott House. Janey took him to see the printers at work and, over lunch, he bought the first copy – "I asked him 'What do you mean to do with these books?' He said, 'To sell them of course.' 'Will you sell this copy to me?' 'Certainly.' 'How much?' 'A pound.' So I paid a pound and took it away."

Morris followed the "Golden" type with "Troy", a black letter Gothic type, which was much nearer his heart than the classical Roman face, and it was with a reduced version of this, "Chaucer", completed by 1894, that he printed the greatest achievement of the Press, *The Kelmscott Chaucer* between August 1894 and May 1896. *The Chaucer* was a collaboration between Morris and Burne-Jones for the two were now friends again and the Sunday breakfasts recommenced. Burne-Jones forgave Morris his politics and Morris, when Ned accepted a Baronetcy in 1894, forgave Burne-Jones. "My husband refused to believe it at first", Jane wrote to Blunt, "but afterwards when the plain fact was known, he said, 'Well, a man can be an ass for the sake of his children.'"

Edward Burne-Jones designed 87 woodcuts for *The Kelmscott Chaucer* each of which was surrounded by an elaborate foliate border by Morris. The subscription list for the 425 paper copies at 20 guineas each and the 13 printed on vellum, priced at 120 guineas, was closed before printing began. The Kelmscott Press books were sought after by dealers and collectors, and once again Morris found himself catering for "the swinish luxury of the rich".

These were happy years for Morris who was now free from much of the administration of his business and released from the exhausting schedule of his socialist crusade. He could spend his time doing the things he enjoyed, writing romances, designing fabrics and making beautiful books. The press provided him with daily excitement and stimulation and there was an echo of the days at Red House because he was

left MAY MORRIS, HENRY HALLIDAY SPARLING, EMERY WALKER AND GEORGE BERNARD SHAW, PHOTOGRAPHED AT KELMSCOTT HOUSE IN THE EARLY 1890s.

above THE FIRST COLOPHON OF THE
KELMSCOTT PRESS, DESIGNED BY
MORRIS IN 1890. THE BACKGROUND IS
NOTICEABLY SIMILAR TO THAT OF THE
DEMOCRATIC FEDERATION
MEMBERSHIP CARD.

surrounded by friends in a collaborative, creative endeavour. Emery Walker, who had refused a partnership, was nonetheless a major contributor to the success of the Press and his advice was readily available, for his own business was conducted from Sussex House, adjoining Sussex Cottage which housed one of Morris's Albion presses; opposite, at 15 Upper Mall, Cobden-Sanderson ran the Doves Bindery. FS Ellis, who edited many of the Kelmscott books, had retired to Torquay but often visited, staying with his son at Hammersmith Terrace, where May now lived, a short walk away, and there was regular contact with Ned and Georgie. Even his relationship with Janey had settled into a comfortable friendship, which Sidney Cockerell, who had succeeded Sparling as Secretary to the Press in 1894, observed one evening as he left Kelmscott House – "When I went up into the drawing room to say goodnight, W.M. and Mrs. M. were playing at draughts, with very large pieces, red and white, Mrs. M. had on a gorgeous blue gown, and they looked like a King and Queen in some old manuscript."

At the end of 1895 Morris was ill and spent November convalescing in Rottingdean on the Sussex coast. He was beginning to look frail, losing weight, and his great unruly mop of hair was now completely white. He was still writing, completing the trilogy of fantasies which began with *The Wood beyond the World* in 1894. On 21 February 1895, Burne-

Jones accompanied his ailing friend to a consultation with Sir William Broadbent, a leading physician, who diagnosed diabetes and further complications. On 28 March, Blunt "found Mrs. Morris very happy, for he was very much better. He was having his supper – oysters etc." But the respite was brief, five days later Morris told Webb that he was "weak and belly-achy."

On 2 June he received one of the first two copies of the *Chaucer*, in a binding by Cobden-Sanderson to Morris's design, but later in the month he was an invalid again, down in Folkestone for the sea air. On 6 July he was cheered by the purchase of the *Windmill Psalter* for £1,000, the largest sum he ever spent on an illuminated manuscript, but later in the month, on the advice of his doctors and against his better judgement, he took a cruise to Norway. He was back by the 18 August when he wrote to Webb, "P.S. Somewhat better, but hated the voyage; so glad to be home."

He was now too weak to write but completed *The Sundering Flood* on 8 September by dictating to Cockerell; on the next morning he signed his will. Three days later Cobden-Sanderson wrote in his diary – "Morris is dying, slowly. It is an astonishing spectacle. He sits speechless, waiting for the end to come." Much to his anguish he was now too feeble to be taken to Kelmscott Manor and knew that he would die in London, far from the meadows, streams and woods about the Upper Thames. Arnold Dolmetsch, a leading figure in the revival of early music, played for him on the virginals, but as the plaintive tones of Byrd and Tallis filled the room, Morris was too overcome by emotion to allow him to continue.

On 28 September, Blunt paid a visit to Hammersmith and Morris "came in like a man risen from the grave, and sat a few minutes at the table, but seemed dazed and unable to follow the conversation. Miss De Morgan was there and his wife, waiting on him...he seemed absorbed in his misery." On Friday 2 October, Morris could not recognize his oldest friend Burne-Jones.

William Morris died on the morning of Saturday 3 October 1896, in his bedroom at his London home, Kelmscott House, Hammersmith. He was 62 years old.

below WILLIAM MORRIS ON HIS DEATHBED, DRAWN BY CHARLES FAIRFAX MURRAY AT KELMSCOTT HOUSE ON 3 OCTOBER 1896.

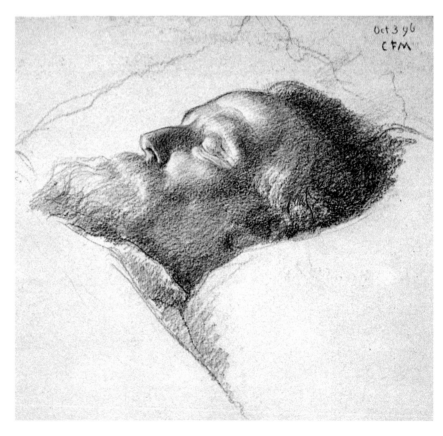

WILLIAM MORRIS AND FOOD

Following a lecture on art in the home, Morris was asked to suggest a suitable decoration for a kitchen. *"Well"*, he said, *"to begin with I think a flitch of bacon suspended from the ceiling is a very good decoration for a kitchen."*

B Y ALL ACCOUNTS MORRIS WAS AN excellent and generous host. Indeed Georgiana Burne-Jones wrote, "It was the most beautiful sight in the world to see Morris coming up from the cellar before dinner, beaming with joy, with his hands full of bottles of wine and others tucked under his arms". Despite his aversion to Society, William Morris was a gregarious man who delighted in the company of his friends. "Fellowship", he told the young socialist Bruce Glasier in the 1880s, "is life, and lack of fellowship is death", a sentiment held since his undergraduate days.

He loved food and drink and the "slim boy" first encountered by Philip Webb in 1856, soon grew into the distinctly tubby figure immortalized in caricature by his friend Burne-Jones. Unlike Bernard Shaw, Morris was unfussy about his diet, and an appreciative guest. In the 1880s, he stayed in Glasgow with Bruce Glasier and his mother during one of his Socialist tours of Scotland. "She had wondered what to make ready for breakfast, but I had assured her that he was not 'faddy' about his food...So she had made him a fine ashetful of our own favourite Sunday morning dish, to wit, ham, eggs, sausage and haddock with home-baked scones and oat-cake. He enjoyed the menu greatly, and said so and he ate quite heartily, which rejoiced her heart."

Morris was a connoisseur of wine and in the early days of The Firm supplied his partners whose accounts were debited for the cases they purchased. Burne-Jones bought 276 bottles in 1869, the year in which the cautious business manager, Warington Taylor, tried and failed to restrict Morris to seven bottles a week. Morris was a valued customer of his wine merchant Mr Diosy and added to his own considerable purchases by supplying his mother. "I have told Diosy to send you 2 dozen only of the claret I use as I think you had better see how it will do before ordering more", he wrote to her on 4 May 1885, "Diosy is not a sherry man and I am rather puzzled as to where you get sherry from". Diosy rewarded his loyalty by sending the family a large pie at Christmas.

Although he was later to maintain that, "A hunk of bread and an onion was a meal for any man", he had a gourmet's interest in food. According to his biographer Mackail, "His taste was more French than modern English", and he abhorred the habit of over-cooking vegetables. A friend who had stayed with Morris for several days, "confessed that he could not remember that they had talked of anything but eating", and Burne-Jones, eavesdropping on his friend's conversation with the distinguished politician John Bright, heard him say, "Yes, yes, there's no doubt about it, a pike should be eaten with a pudding in its innards."

Unlike many of his contemporaries, Morris actually knew about and enjoyed cooking, an interest fostered in childhood when he was familiar with the dairy, bakery and brewery of his father's estate, Woodford Hall.

previous page left A TRUG FILLED WITH FRESH VEGETABLES OUTSIDE KELMSCOTT MANOR.

previous page right MORRIS AT DINNER WITH PHILIP AND EDWARD BURNE-JONES. A CARICATURE BY EDWARD BURNE-JONES.

While living there he also played in the orchards and kitchen garden; roasted the rabbits, redwing and fieldfare which he shot with his younger brother, and spent happy hours fishing for pike and perch, the recreation which gave him the most pleasure for the rest of his life. "I wouldn't at all mind being a cook", he declared, adding, with uncharacteristic chauvinism, "There are two things about which women know absolutely nothing, dress and cookery...They have no sense of colour or grace in drapery, and they never invented a new dish or failed to half spoil an old one."

As the Morris's employed several servants he had few opportunities to indulge in practical cookery but when he did, the results usually met with approval. In July 1871, trekking through Iceland with Faulkner and Magnusson, he cooked a stew of four curlews, lean bacon and tinned carrots which he declared a great success. Nine years later, on a summer boat trip, the Hon. Richard Grosvenor reported that Morris cooked "very thick soup, rice, vegetables, meat etc. – results showing both knowledge and skill", and Glasier recalled a picnic in 1889 with, "Rolls of bread and pats of butter, veal and ham pies, boiled eggs, nuts and pears and a delectable salad compounded by his own hands."

Occasionally, however, he had to confess to culinary failures. "I have done some cooking, my dear," he wrote to his daughter Jenny in 1888, "with not very startling success. 1st. An Irish stew; all right except that the meat was rather tough; but I shall know better another time: 2nd. A hash of somewhat tough fowl – made it tougher you bet – 3rd. fried the perch for breakfast yesterday: they were done and were not greasy but not properly crisp: you see I am out of practice my dear: also I come to the conclusion that cooking takes a very long time to do; and I can better understand why the British working man's family is so bad at it – and I look with respectful wonder on the French ditto who is so good at it."

left WILLIAM MORRIS EATING FISH IN ICELAND, ONE OF MANY CARICATURES OF MORRIS EATING BY BURNE-JONES.

SOUPS AND STARTERS

FRESH PEA, LETTUCE AND MINT SOUP Serves 4-6

A light summery soup made with ingredients fresh from a country garden.

1½ oz/40 g butter
1 large onion, chopped
2 celery stalks, diced
2½ pts/1.25 litres light stock or water
1 cos or 2 small round soft lettuce,
leaves roughly torn
1¼ lb/625 g fresh shelled peas
2 tsp fresh thyme leaves
about 4 tsp chopped fresh mint
1 oz/25 g plain flour
salt and freshly ground black pepper
a little lemon juice

TO SERVE
double or soured cream or yogurt
torn mint leaves

Melt half of the butter in a large saucepan. Add the onion and celery and cook gently for 5 minutes, stirring frequently until softened. Do not brown. Add the stock or water and bring to the boil. When boiling add the lettuce and 1 lb/500 g of the peas together with the thyme and mint. Return to the boil then lower the heat, cover and simmer for 20 minutes. Allow to cool slightly then purée and pass through a sieve. In a clean pan melt the remaining butter, stir in the flour and make a roux. Cook for 1 minute. Gradually add the puréed pea mixture, stirring well to keep the mixture smooth. Bring to the boil and season to taste with salt, pepper and a squeeze of lemon juice. Add a little more fresh mint to taste if you wish. Add the remaining peas, lower the heat and simmer the soup for 8-10 minutes until they are tender.

Serve the soup swirled with a little cream, soured cream or yogurt, with shredded fresh mint leaves to garnish.

HAM AND LENTIL SOUP Serves 4-6

1 ham joint on the bone, weighing
about 1½ lb/675 g
1 onion, halved and studded
with 2 cloves
1 carrot
8 peppercorns
1 oz/25 g butter
1 large onion, chopped
2 carrots, finely diced
2 celery stalks, finely diced
1 medium potato, diced
12 oz/350 g red lentils
1 bay leaf
sprig of thyme
salt and freshly ground black pepper
chopped parsley, to serve

First prepare the ham stock. Put the ham joint in a large pan, cover with water and bring to the boil. Boil for 1 minute then discard the salty cooking water.

Add 3 pts/2.5 litres of fresh cold water to the pan with onion, carrot and peppercorns. Return to the boil then lower the heat, cover and simmer for 1½ hours until the ham is tender.

Transfer the ham to a plate and leave to cool slightly, then flake it with a fork and set aside. Leave the stock to cool, then skim the fat from the surface and strain. Set aside.

Melt the butter in a large saucepan on medium heat. Add the vegetables and cook, stirring for 5-6 minutes to soften. Stir in the lentils, bay and thyme and add the reserved ham stock. Bring to the boil and then lower the heat, cover and simmer for 1¼ hours, until the lentils and vegetables have broken down to a thick pulpy soup.

Add the flaked ham to the soup and adjust the seasoning to taste. Continue cooking the soup for a further 15 minutes. Lift out and discard the bay leaf and thyme sprig. Serve piping hot, sprinkled with chopped parsley.

right PEA, LETTUCE AND MINT SOUP

SPATCHCOCKED PIGEONS WITH MUSTARD SAUCE Serves 4

2 young pigeons
2 oz/50 g soft butter
1 oz/25 g fresh white breadcrumbs
½ tsp paprika
½ tsp ground mace
salt and freshly ground black pepper

SAUCE
1 oz/25 g butter
1 large or 2 small shallots, finely chopped
1 clove garlic, crushed
large glass
dry white wine
juice of 1 orange
1 tbsp Dijon mustard

TO SERVE
4 slices hot buttered toast

Cut the pigeons along their backbones and open out flat, pressing down hard on the breastbones. Rub all over with the soft butter. Season the breadcrumbs with paprika, mace, salt and freshly ground black pepper and use to coat the birds.

Cook the pigeons under a preheated hot grill, starting skin-side down, for about 5 minutes each side.

Meanwhile to prepare the sauce, melt the butter in a heavy frying pan. Add the shallot and garlic and cook on a medium high heat for 5 minutes until soft but not browned. Raise the heat and pour in the glass of wine. Let it bubble until it is reduced by about half, then lower the heat and add the orange juice and mustard. Simmer for a few minutes and season to taste.

To serve, use poultry scissors or a heavy knife to cut the birds in half along the breastbone. Serve each piece of pigeon on hot buttered toast with a little of the mustard sauce poured over and a sprinkling of chopped parsley to finish.

CHEESE BALLS Makes 15-20 balls

This is a recipe that May Morris used, taken directly from her cookbook.

2 egg whites
2 oz/50 g finely grated parmesan cheese
¼ tsp cayenne pepper
salt
oil for deep frying
a little extra grated parmesan, for sprinkling

Whisk the egg whites until stiff and fold in the parmesan cheese. Season with cayenne and a little salt. Heat oil for frying (temperature 170°C /335°F when a bread cube should brown in 1½ minutes).

Shape spoonfuls of the mixture into marble-sized balls and drop them, a few at a time, into the hot fat. Cook for 2-3 minutes until crisp and golden. Drain well and serve hot, piled on a warmed plate with a little extra cheese sprinkled over.

right SPATCHCOCKED PIGEONS WITH MUSTARD SAUCE

FRIED OYSTERS WITH BACON

Serves 4

For an elegant starter, here are fried oysters with small rolls of bacon, served with fried bread, lemon and chopped parsley.

In a large frying pan poach the oysters in their own liquor for 1 minute to set. Leave to cool. Dip in seasoned flour then egg and then breadcrumbs to coat. Set aside.

In a large frying pan fry the bread triangles in a little of the oil and butter until golden. Cook the bacon rolls under a hot grill until browned and crisping. Keep both hot.

In a large frying pan, heat the remaining oil and butter until very hot. Add the oysters and fry quickly for just 1 minute to brown and crisp. Take care not to overcook.

Serve the oysters sprinkled with chopped parsley and with lemon wedges for squeezing. Accompany with bacon rolls and bread triangles.

12 large oysters (3 per person)
flour seasoned with salt and pepper,
for coating
1 egg, beaten
2 oz/50 g dried white breadcrumbs
2 oz/50 g butter
5 tbsp corn oil
4 slices bread, crusts removed and
cut into triangles

BACON ROLLS
6 slices dry cured bacon, halved,
stretched and rolled tightly

TO SERVE
finely chopped parsley
lemon wedges

left FRESH OYSTERS
far left FRIED OYSTERS WITH BACON

MEAT DISHES

IRISH STEW Serves 4-6

12 lamb cutlets
2 large onions, sliced
2 lb/1 kg potatoes, peeled and sliced
salt and pepper
1-1½ pts/600-900 ml stock

TO SERVE
chopped parsley

Trim the cutlets neatly, removing any excess fat. Brown in a shallow pan. In a heavy flameproof casserole layer the meat, onions and potatoes, seasoning between the layers and finishing with a layer of potatoes. Pour in the stock (to half fill the casserole). Cover and heat until simmering. Lower the heat and cook very gently for 2-2½ hours. Alternatively cook, covered, in a preheated oven at 190°C/375°F/Gas 5 for 2½ hours. Remove the lid and cook uncovered for the last 20 minutes. Serve sprinkled with chopped parsley.

SALTED AND SPICED COLD BEEF ROAST Serves 6-8

Beef preserved by salting is not so easy to come across today but it is relatively easy to prepare given a fair amount of forward planning (the spicing process takes about a week), and a cold roast of spiced beef is a delicious change from a cooked ham.

5 lb/2½ kg plus piece of silverside,
rump or brisket
4 oz/125 g soft brown sugar

SALT AND SPICE MIXTURE
1 oz/25 g allspice berries
1 oz/25 g juniper berries
1 oz/25 g black peppercorns
½ oz/15 g whole coriander seeds
1 piece nutmeg, grated
8 whole cloves
4 oz/125 g salt

TO BRAISE
2 tbsp oil
2 carrots, chopped
2 celery stalks, chopped
1 onion, chopped
1 clove garlic, chopped

Make this with a large joint – not less than 5 lb/2½ kg – so it will feed a number of guests or last a few days.
Put the beef in a close-fitting dish and sprinkle over the sugar. Cover tightly and leave in a cool place for 2 days, turning two or three times. To prepare the spice mixture, coarsely grind all the spices together using a grinder, or pound them in a mortar. Mix them with the salt. Remove the meat from the sugar and rub all over with the spice mixture. Cover and leave in a cool place for about 5 days, turning and rubbing in the spices every day. A larger piece of meat will require longer spicing – up to 8 days for the flavour to penetrate.
For braising, preheat the oven to 150°C/300°F/Gas 2. Heat the oil in a flameproof casserole large enough to hold the beef. Add the vegetables and garlic and sauté gently for 10 minutes until lightly browned. Remove the beef from the spice mixture and wipe clean. Place on top of the vegetables and add water to a depth of about 1 in/2.5 cm. Cover tightly with a lid and foil and bake in the oven for 25-30 minutes per 1 lb/500 g plus 30 minutes until tender.
When the beef is cooked, remove it from the casserole and wrap tightly in foil. Stand it on a board and place a second board on top. Cover this with a weight and leave overnight before serving.
Serve slices with salads, pickles and mustards, or in sandwiches.

right IRISH STEW

VEAL AND HAM PIE Serves 4-6

HOT WATER CRUST PASTRY
1 lb/500 g plain flour
1 tsp salt
8 oz/250 g lard
¼ pt/150 ml water

FILLING
2 lb/1 kg English Veal,
diced into ½ in/1 cm cubes
1 tbsp flour
2 tsp chopped fresh thyme
finely grated zest of 1 lemon
4 tbsp white wine or vermouth
salt and freshly ground black pepper
1 lb/500 g ham, diced into
½ in/1 cm cubes
4 tbsp chopped fresh parsley
1 tsp freshly grated nutmeg

TO GLAZE
1 egg yolk beaten with 1 tbsp water

To prepare the pastry, sieve the flour and salt into a mixing bowl and make a well in the centre. Put the lard (or half lard and half butter) into a saucepan with the water. Heat until just boiling and then tip into the flour, stirring with a wooden spoon. Beat well to form a smooth dough then turn on to a floured surface and knead gently. Leave to rest and cool slightly for 10 minutes.

Preheat the oven to 220°C/442°F/Gas 7.

Meanwhile to prepare the filling, in a bowl mix together the veal cubes, flour, thyme, lemon zest and white wine or vermouth. Season with salt and freshly ground black pepper. In a separate bowl mix the ham, parsley, nutmeg and season as before.

Roll out three-quarters of the pastry and use to line a 2 lb/1 kg loaf tin or pie mould (a long narrow shape is preferable for slicing). Spoon half the veal mixture into the base and press down lightly with a metal spoon. Cover with the ham and them layer the remaining veal on top, pressing down to level and fill the tin. Dampen the pastry edges with a little water and roll out the remaining pastry to form a lid. Use scissors to snip small vents along the top of the pie.

Bake the pie in the centre of the oven for 15 minutes and then lower the temperature to 180°C/350°F/Gas 4 and continue cooking for 1½ hours. Cool slightly and brush on the glaze of egg yolk and water. Chill, preferably overnight, before carefully turning out onto a serving dish. Serve cut into thick slices.

FRIED STEAKS WITH DEVILLED HERB BUTTER Serves 4

DEVILLED HERB BUTTER
4 oz/125 g softened butter
¼ tsp cayenne pepper
3 tbsp chopped fresh mixed herbs
½ clove garlic, crushed
a few drops lemon juice
freshly ground black pepper
4 steaks, 6-8 oz/175-250 g each
1 tbsp oil
½ oz/15 g butter

right VEAL AND HAM PIE

First make the devilled herb butter. Blend all the ingredients together in a small bowl, using the back of a wooden spoon to pound the mixture well. Shape into small pats and chill until firm.

Trim the steaks and wipe dry. Beat each steak lightly on both sides with a steak mallet or rolling pin. Season with pepper (but no salt as this causes the juices to run during cooking).

Heat the oil and butter together in a large frying pan until hot and sizzling. Add the steaks and cook on a high heat until browned on one side and then flip over to brown the other side. Lower the heat and continue cooking until done as required. This will take about 4 minutes for rare steak, up to 10 minutes for well done. Serve the steaks at once, topped with pats of Devilled Herb Butter.

LAMB IN CLARET Serves 4

Spike each of the lamb noisettes with a rosemary sprig and season on both sides with pepper. Heat together the oil and butter in a large heavy frying pan. Add the lamb and cook on a high heat turning once or twice until browned on the outside and tender and pink inside. Remove to a plate and keep hot.

Add the garlic to the pan and pour in the claret. Cook on a fairly high heat scraping up all the sediment in the pan. Stir in the redcurrant jelly and continue cooking until the sauce is reduced by almost half. Add a squeeze of lemon juice. Season with salt and freshly ground black pepper to taste. Spoon the sauce over the lamb and serve with rosemary spikes and fine green beans.

8 lamb noisettes (1 in/2.5 cm thick)
8 small sprigs rosemary
freshly ground black pepper
1 tbsp oil
1 oz/25 g butter
1 clove garlic, crushed
½ pt/300 ml claret
3 tbsp redcurrant or other fruit jelly
squeeze of lemon juice
salt

TO SERVE
rosemary spikes
fine green beans

ROAST DUCK WITH ROOT VEGETABLES Serves 4

Preheat the oven to 200°C/400°F/Gas 6.

Using a skewer or a needle prick the skin of the duck all over to let the fat run during cooking. Season the bird well with salt and pepper and place it on a rack. Set in a roasting tin. Cover loosely with foil and roast for 1¼ hours removing the foil halfway through cooking to allow the skin to brown and crisp. Remove about 4 tbsp of the duck fat from the roasting tin and reserve.

About 40 minutes before the end of cooking time prepare the sauce. Heat 2 tbsp of the reserved duck fat in a medium saucepan. Add the shallots and cook gently for 7-8 minutes until soft and just starting to brown. Stir in the white wine and bring to the boil. Let the mixture bubble and evaporate for a minute then add the orange zest, juice, and stock. Bring to a simmer and cook gently for 10 minutes then add the Marsala. Turn up the heat and reduce the sauce by about one-third. Season to taste and set aside.

Heat the remaining 2 tbsp duck fat in a large heavy frying pan. Add the vegetables and cook stirring over a medium heat for 2 minutes. Add the orange juice, sugar and seasoning to the pan and bring just to the boil. Cook, uncovered on a medium heat stirring frequently for about 10 minutes until the liquid has evaporated and caramelized to a glaze and the vegetables are tender.

Serve the duck on a warmed platter surrounded by the glazed vegetables. Reheat the sauce to accompany.

1 oven-ready duckling, about
3½ lb/1.5 kg
salt and freshly ground black pepper
1 lb/500 g small carrots or parsnips,
halved lengthwise
12 oz/375 g baby turnips
juice of 1 orange
3 tsp brown sugar

SAUCE
2 shallots
¼ pt/150 ml dry white wine
1 tsp finely grated orange zest
juice of 1 orange
¼ pt/150 ml chicken stock
4 tbsp Marsala

left LAMB IN CLARET

STEW OF RABBIT WITH APPLE AND PRUNES Serves 4

1 rabbit, jointed
4 tbsp plain flour seasoned with salt and pepper
1 oz/25 g butter
3 tbsp sunflower or light olive oil
2 onions, sliced
3 rashers of bacon, cut into squares
½ pt/300 ml light stock
sprig of fresh thyme
2 small cooking apples
4 oz/125 g prunes
chopped parsley, to serve

Wipe the rabbit pieces dry with kitchen paper and coat with the seasoned flour. Heat the butter and oil in a flameproof casserole or heavy pan until sizzling, add the rabbit pieces, in two batches if necessary, and brown on all sides. Remove the joints to a plate. Add the onion to the pan and cook for a few minutes to soften, then stir in the bacon. Pour in the stock and scrape up the bits on the base of the pan. Return the rabbit to the pan with the thyme. Cover and cook gently for 1 hour, then add the apples and prunes to the stew. Cook covered for a further 30-45 minutes until the rabbit is tender. Adjust the seasoning and serve hot, sprinkled with chopped parsley.

FISH DISHES

SOHO COD Serves 2

Here is another recipe from May Morris's cookbook.

2 cod steaks, about 1 in/2.5 cm thick, or thick piece of fillet
a little butter, for greasing
4 spring onions, finely chopped
1 tbsp chopped parsley
juice of ½ lemon
½ pt/300 ml water
1 tbsp flour
1 oz/25 g butter
salt and freshly ground black pepper
boiled rice, to serve

Preheat the oven to 190°C/375°F/Gas 5.
Place the cod in a buttered baking tin (choose one which will go on the hob as well as in the oven). Sprinkle with the chopped spring onions, parsley and lemon juice. Pour the water around and loosely cover with a sheet of buttered greaseproof paper or parchment. Bake in the oven for about 20 minutes until the fish is firm and flakes easily. Remove the fish to a serving plate and keep hot.
Mix together the flour and butter to form a paste. Set the baking tin on top of the cooker on a medium heat. Add the butter mixture in small pieces, mixing well to form a thickened sauce. Season with salt and pepper and spoon over the fish to serve. Accompany with boiled rice.

GRILLED HALIBUT STEAKS Serves 4

This is adapted from a recipe for Broiled Brill by May Morris. It's a simple marinade recipe which flavours the halibut steaks and keeps them moist during grilling, or `broiling' if you prefer.

4 halibut steaks
3 tbsp salad oil
juice of ½ lemon
¼ tsp cayenne pepper
salt and freshly ground black pepper

Wash and trim the fish and dry it well with a cloth. Put the salad oil, lemon juice, cayenne and seasoning in a deep plate. Dip the fish into the marinade and cook under a hot grill for about 8 minutes, turning once. During cooking brush the fish with any remaining marinade.

right GRILLED HALIBUT STEAKS

FRIED TROUT WITH ALMONDS AND FIELD MUSHROOMS Serves 4

You'd be very fortunate indeed to catch your own trout and on the same occasion pick a handful of wild mushrooms to cook with them for supper. However, the combination of the two ingredients is a glorious one.

2 oz/50 g butter
2 oz/50 g blanched almonds
4 trout, cleaned
1 oz/25 g flour, seasoned with salt and pepper
1 lb/500 g field mushrooms, sliced if large
2 tbsp chopped parsley
juice of ½ lemon
Split the almonds lengthwise

Melt half the butter (1 oz/25 g) in a large frying pan. Add the almonds and cook for 2 minutes on a medium high heat, stirring, until browned on all sides. Remove to a plate.

Rub the fish all over with seasoned flour. Add the remaining 1 oz/25 g of the butter to the pan and fry the fish, two at a time for 3-4 minutes each side until cooked through. Transfer to a serving platter or individual plates and keep hot.

Fry the mushrooms quickly in the pan and when almost done, return the almonds to the pan with the parsley and lemon juice. Shake over the heat until hot and sizzling, then spoon over the fish.

BAKED PIKE WITH FORCEMEAT STUFFING Serves 4

FORCEMEAT
8 oz/250 g minced veal or chicken
2 tbsp chopped mixed herbs, eg from parsley, thyme, fennel, chervil
1 small onion, finely chopped
½ clove garlic, crushed
3 oz/75 g fresh white breadcrumbs
1 tsp finely grated lemon zest
1 egg yolk
salt and freshly ground black pepper

2½ - 3 lb/1¼ - 1½ kg pike, cleaned
a little flour
2 oz/50 g butter
1 glass red wine
juice of 1 large orange

Preheat the oven to 190°C/375°F/Gas 5.

Mix together the ingredients for the forcemeat, adding plenty of salt and pepper.

Rinse and dry the fish and fill the cavity with the forcemeat stuffing. Rub all over with flour and seasoning and place in a large shallow baking dish which has been greased well with some of the butter.

Pour the red wine and orange juice around the fish and dot the remaining butter over the top.

Bake in the oven for about 35 minutes, basting the fish frequently with the juices. The flesh should be firm and opaque and flake easily from the backbone when cooked.

Serve the fish with a little stuffing and the juices spooned around.

right FRIED TROUT WITH ALMONDS AND FIELD MUSHROOMS

VEGETABLES

SPRING VEGETABLE SALAD Serves 4

Choose whatever looks glorious in the garden or market to make this colourful salad of crisply cooked vegetables. Add herbs and leaves such as lettuce hearts, rocket, dandelion, salad burnet or nasturtium for flavour and texture.

To prepare the dressing, mix all the ingredients together and set aside to allow the flavours to develop and mingle.

To prepare the asparagus, use a potato peeler to pare about 2 ins/5 cm of peel from the base of the stalks. Add the spears to boiling water in a shallow pan and cook for 3 minutes, then drain and refresh under cold running water. Drain thoroughly and set aside.

Boil the potatoes until tender then drain and leave to cool.

Trim all the other vegetables and cook briefly, then drain and refresh as for the asparagus.

To serve, arrange the vegetables and salad leaves on a large platter. Scatter over the herbs and season with sea salt and freshly ground black pepper. Serve the dressing in a separate dish for spooning.

DRESSING
6 tbsp mayonnaise
6 tbsp soured cream
whites of 2 spring onions finely chopped
3 tbsp chopped fresh herbs such as parsley, chives, tarragon and dill
salt and freshly ground black pepper

1 bundle of asparagus
8 oz/250 g small new potatoes
1 small bunch baby carrots
1 small bunch baby turnips
6 oz/175 g fine green beans
6 oz/175 g runner beans, cut into short lengths
salad leaves and fresh herbs such as lettuce hearts, salad burnet, mache, rocket, chives, chervil, dill and mint
coarse sea salt and pepper

BAKED CABBAGE WITH APPLES AND RAISINS Serves 4

You can also make this slow-baked cabbage dish using a hard white or red cabbage, both of which should be allowed a little extra time in the oven.

Preheat the oven to 150°C/300°F/Gas 2.

Shred the cabbage finely. Peel, core and halve the apples, then cut into thin slices and toss them in the lemon juice to prevent discolouring. Use some of the butter to grease an oven-proof casserole dish and fill with the cabbage, apple, onion and raisins in layers so they are evenly mixed. Season with salt and freshly ground black pepper. Add 2 tablespoons of water to the dish, cover and bake in the oven for 1¼ -1½ hours until tender. Remove the lid, dot the cabbage with the remaining butter and season with freshly grated nutmeg, then return to the oven for a final 15 minutes before serving.

1 large Savoy cabbage
2 Bramley apples
juice of ½ lemon
2 oz/50 g butter
1 large onion, sliced
2 oz/50 g raisins
salt and freshly ground black pepper
freshly grated nutmeg

left SPRING VEGETABLE SALAD

DESSERTS AND CAKES

RICH LIGHT FRUIT CAKE Makes 8 slices

*4 oz/125 g luxury glacé fruits eg
pineapple, cherries, plums, peel
8 oz/250 g self-raising flour
1 tsp baking powder
½ tsp salt
4 oz/125 g sultanas
8 oz/250 g butter
8 oz/250 g light muscovado sugar
4 eggs, beaten
1 tbsp milk or brandy*

Grease and line an 8 in/20 cm deep, loose-bottomed cake tin. Preheat the oven to 180°C/350°F/Gas 4.

Cut the glacé fruits into small pieces. Put in a sieve and rinse thoroughly under warm running water to remove all stickiness. Dry thoroughly on a clean tea towel.

Sieve together the flour, baking powder and salt and stir in the glacé fruit and sultanas.

In a separate bowl, cream together the butter and sugar until light and fluffy. Add the eggs, gradually, beating well. If the mixture begins to curdle beat in a little of the flour. Fold the flour and fruit mixture into the egg mixture, together with the milk or brandy.

Spoon the mixture into the prepared tin and smooth the top making a slight hollow in the centre. Bake in the oven for 30 minutes then lower the oven temperature to 160°C/275°F/Gas 3 and continue baking for about 40 minutes until firm. Cool in the tin slightly before turning out.

POACHED PEARS WITH BRAMBLES OR MULBERRIES Serves 6

Any firm pears can be used for this recipe – Williams and Conference are good, but if using Williams they work best if slightly under-ripe. Served warm with crisp biscuits to dip into the syrup, or chilled with thick cream or vanilla ice.

*6 firm ripe pears
½ lemon
4 oz/125 g sugar
1 bottle sweet dessert wine
1 cinnamon stick
4 cloves
shredded zest and juice of 1 orange
or lemon
8 oz/250 g fresh blackberries or
mulberries*

Peel the pears, keeping the stalk intact. If you like, remove the core from the base of the pear. Rub the cut surface of the lemon over the pears to prevent them discolouring.

Put the sugar and wine into a saucepan just large enough to hold the pears. Snap the cinnamon stick in two and add to the pan with the cloves. Bring the syrup to the boil, stirring at first to dissolve the sugar. Add the pears and bring to a gentle simmer. Allow to poach very gently for 30-40 minutes until the pears are tender and translucent. The exact cooking time will depend on the ripeness of the pears.

Transfer the cooked pears to a serving dish, leaving the syrup in the pan. Increase the heat and boil the syrup for 5 minutes, then add the citrus zest and juice and about half of the berries to the pan, breaking them up a little with a wooden spoon. Continue to boil the syrup for a few more minutes until it is slightly thickened. Serve warm or cold with the remaining blackberries or mulberries.

right POACHED PEARS WITH BRAMBLES OR MULBERRIES

VANILLA CUSTARD TART WITH FRESH CURRANTS Serves 6-8

PASTRY
8 oz/225 g/ plain flour
pinch of salt
3 oz/75 g sugar
4 oz/125 g butter, softened, plus
extra for greasing
1 egg
grated zest of 1 lemon

CUSTARD FILLING
1 egg
2 egg yolks
1 oz/25 g sugar
¾ pt/450 ml cream
1 tsp vanilla essence
10 oz/300 g fresh currants
icing, caster or vanilla sugar,
for dusting

Sift the flour, salt and sugar into a bowl and work in the butter with the fingertips. Make a well in the centre and add the egg and lemon zest. Gradually bring the flour in from the edges, mixing to a smooth dough. Leave to rest for 20 minutes.

Preheat the oven to 180°C/350°F/Gas 4. Grease a 10 in/25 cm tart tin with a little butter.

Roll out the pastry on a floured surface and use it to line the tart tin. There is no need to remove any overhang. Chill briefly until firm and then line with baking paper or foil and bake blind for 10 minutes. Remove the paper or foil, trim the edges and return to the oven for a further 10 minutes.

Meanwhile prepare the custard filling. Put the egg, egg yolks and sugar in a bowl and beat well. In a small saucepan, heat the cream until almost boiling and then pour onto the egg mixture, whisking constantly. Stir in the vanilla essence. Strain the mixture into the cooked tart shell. Bake in the oven for about 20 minutes until the centre is lightly set. Remove the tart from the oven but leave in the tin until cold. To finish, pile the currants on top of the custard and dust with sugar.

STRAWBERRIES À LA MORRIS

The gardens at Red House were a source of abundant fruit, much of which was used in the household's cooking.

Simply choose some attractive leaves from a cabbage and wash and pat dry the leaves and the strawberries. Pile the fruit into the leaves and give each guest an individual package.

ELDERBERRY SYRUP

Delicious on ice cream or yogurt and spooned over other puddings, this syrup can also be added to sauces and glazes. For a refreshing drink dilute with soda and serve iced with mint. This is adapted from May Morris's cookbook.

1 lb/500 g ripe elderberries
1 lb/500 g caster sugar
strip of lemon peel
1 almond, shredded

Put all the ingredients into a saucepan with 1 pt/600 ml water. Bring to the boil then lower the heat a little and allow to bubble for 1 hour. Leave to cool. When quite cold, strain the syrup and transfer to a sterilized bottle for keeping. If you prefer a thicker syrup, boil it up again after it has been cooled and strain to reduce it further.

right STRAWBERRIES À LA MORRIS AND VANILLA CUSTARD TART WITH FRESH CURRANTS

APPLE AMBER Serves 4

APPLE PUREE
2¼ lb/1 kg Bramley or other
cooking apples
grated zest and juice of 1 lemon
3 oz/75 g soft light brown sugar
1 tsp ground cinnamon
pinch of ground cloves or 2
whole cloves

3 eggs, separated
6 oz/175 g caster sugar

TO SERVE
pouring cream

To make the apple purée, peel, core and slice the apples and place in a pan with the lemon zest and juice. Mix well. Stir in the brown sugar, cinnamon and cloves and cook, covered on a medium heat, stirring frequently until the apples soften to a thick purée. Leave to cool slightly and remove the whole cloves if using.

Preheat the oven to 180°C/350°F/Gas 4.

Add the egg yolks to the apple purée and mix well. Transfer to a shallow baking dish (about 2 pt/1 litre capacity) and bake in the oven for 15 minutes.

In a clean bowl whisk the egg whites until they form stiff peaks. Gradually whisk in all but 1 tbsp of the caster sugar. Pile the meringue on top of the hot apple mixture and sprinkle the remaining 1 tbsp sugar on top. Return to the oven for 12-15 minutes until the meringue is golden. Serve with pouring cream.

EGGS IN SNOW Serves 4

This recipe is based on one from May Morris's cookbook at Kelmscott Manor.

3 eggs, separated
5 oz/125 g caster sugar
¾ pt/450 ml milk
1 tsp vanilla essence

Preheat the oven to 160°C/325°F/Gas 3.

In a bowl beat together the egg yolks and 2 oz/50 g of the sugar.

In a small saucepan heat the milk until just boiling. Pour on to the egg yolks and whisk thoroughly. Add the vanilla. Strain into an ovenproof dish (1½ pt/900 ml capacity). Set the dish in a larger dish of boiling water and bake for 40-45 minutes until sightly set.

Whisk the egg whites until stiff, fold in the remaining 3 oz/75 g sugar. Pile on top of the custard. Return to the oven and bake for a further 10 minutes until the meringue is just set.

SEED CAKE Makes 8 slices

12 oz/375 g self-raising flour
pinch of salt
6 oz/175 g butter, diced
6 oz/175 g caster sugar
1 oz/25 g caraway seeds
3 eggs, beaten
about 3 tbsp milk

right SEED CAKE

Preheat the oven to 180°C/350°F/Gas 4.

Grease and line an 8 in/20 cm loose-bottomed deep cake tin.

Sieve the flour and salt into a mixing bowl. Add the butter and rub in until the mixture resembles fine breadcrumbs. Stir in the sugar and caraway seeds. Beat in the eggs using a wooden spoon, adding enough milk to give the mixture a stiff dropping consistency. Spoon into the prepared cake tin and level the surface. Bake in the preheated oven for about 45 minutes until the cake is firm and a skewer inserted into the centre comes out clean. Turn out and cool on a wire rack.

FURTHER READING

ON MORRIS: Kelvin, Norman, ed *The Collected Letters of William Morris* 3 volumes (Princeton, 1984 -)
  MacCarthy, Fiona *William Morris; a life for our time* (London, 1994)
  Mackail, JW *The Life of William Morris* 2 volumes (London, 1899)
  Morris, May *The Introductions to the Collected Works of William Morris* 2 volumes (New York, 1973)
ON BUSINESS: Harvey, C and Press, J *William Morris, Design and enterprise in Victorian Britain* (Manchester, 1991)
ON DESIGNS: Thompson, Paul *The Work of William Morris* (London, 1967)
  Watkinson, Raymond *William Morris as a designer* (London, 1967)
ON POLITICS: Salmon, Nicholas, ed *Political Writings* (Bristol, 1994)
  Thompson, EP *William Morris, Romantic to Revolutionary* (London, 1976)
ON PRINTING: Petersen, William *The Kelmscott Press* (Oxford, 1993)
ON STAINED GLASS: Sewter, AC *The stained glass of William Morris and his circle* 2 volumes (Yale, 1974)
ON TEXTILES: Parry, Linda *William Morris Textiles* (London, 1983)
ON JANE MORRIS: Bryson, J, ed *Dante Gabriel Rossetti and Jane Morris, their correspondence* (Oxford, 1976)
  Faulkner, Peter, ed *Jane Morris to Wilfrid Scawen Blunt* (Exeter, 1968)
  Marsh, Jan *Jane and May Morris* (London, 1986)
ON EDWARD BURNE-JONES: Burne-Jones, Georgiana *Memorials of Edward Burne-Jones* 2 volumes (London, 1904)
  Fitzgerald, Penelope *Edward Burne-Jones, A Biography* (London, 1975)
ON DANTE GABRIEL ROSSETTI: Doughty, Oswald *Victorian Romantic; Dante Gabriel Rossetti* (London, 1949)
  Doughty, O and Wahl, JR, eds *The Letters of Dante Gabriel Rossetti* 4 volumes (Oxford, 1965-7)

WILLIAM MORRIS'S HOUSES

At the time of writing, the following houses in which Morris lived are open to the public. Water House, Lloyd Park, Forest Road, Walthamstow, now houses the William Morris Gallery and is open from Tuesday to Saturday, 10am-1pm and 2-5pm. Red House, Red House Lane, Bexleyheath, Kent, is a private house which may be seen on written application. Kelmscott Manor, Kelmscott, near Lechlade, Gloucestershire, belongs to the Society of Antiquaries but is open to the public on Wednesdays between April and September. Kelmscott House, 26 Upper Mall, Hammersmith, is a private house but the basement and coach house, which are the headquarters of The William Morris Society, are open on Thursdays and Saturdays between 2pm and 5pm.

AUTHOR'S ACKNOWLEDGMENTS

I should like to thank Peter Cormack, Edward Hollamby, Yvonne Jones, Clare Martin and Linda Parry for their help, and friends and colleagues at the William Morris Society for their encouragement. No recent writer on Morris can fail to be indebted to Professor Norman Kelvin whose edition of Morris's *Collected Letters* has proved invaluable. Fiona MacCarthy's biography, *William Morris, a life for our time*, has been an inspiration and I hope that any accidental plagiarism may be seen as a tribute. Although all my major published sources are listed above I should like to acknowledge two specific articles published in *The Journal of The William Morris Society*, "The Expedition of The Ark" by JM Bassius in Volume 111, Number 3, Spring 1977, and "Where Janey used to live" by Margaret Fleming in Volume IV, Number 4, Winter 1981.

INDEX

Italic numbers refer to illustrations.
Bold entries are recipes.

Adams, Rev. WF, 11
All Saint's, Selsey, *50, 53*
Allingham, William, 33, 56, 64, 65
apples: apple amber, 156
  baked cabbage with apples and raisins, 151
Art Workers' Guild, 125

Barratts of Chiswick, 10
Batchelor, Joseph, 127
Bax, Belfort, 118
beef: fried steaks with devilled herb butter, 142
  salted and spiced cold beef roast, 140
Bell, Sir Lothian, 116
Bell and Daldry, 67
blackberries: poached pears with brambles, 152, *153*
Blow, Detmar, 10, 11
Blunt, Wilfrid Scawen, 84, 90, 91, 107-9, 127, 129
Bodley, GF, 53
A Book of Verse, 72, *73*
Bossom, William, 113
Boudichon, Barbara, 71
Bowden, William, 127
Boyce, George, 46, 52, 64
Boyd, Alice, 71
Broadbent, Sir William, 129
Brotherhood, 27
Browning, Robert, 32, 67
Buchanan, Robert, 83
Burden, Anne, 37
Burden, Elizabeth "Bessie", 11, 37, 46, *52*, 56, 62, 64, 65
Burden, Jane, *14*
Burden, Robert, 37
Burne-Jones, Sir Edward, 11, *13, 19*, 23, 27-33, *36*, 44-8, *48*, 51, 56-9, 65, 72, *83, 85, 85*, 90, *94, 101*, 117, 127, 128, *131*, 132, *133*
Burne-Jones, Georgiana, 10, 11, *13*, 33, 44, 46, 47-8, *49*, 56, 59, 70, 72, 94, 132
Burne-Jones, Philip, 51, 56
Burns, John, 11

cabbage, baked with apples and raisins, 151
cakes: rich light fruit cake, **152**
  seed cake, 156, *157*

Campfield, George, 53
Carlyle, Thomas, 27-8, 101
Caxton, William, 125
Chaucer, Geoffrey, 33, 42, 45, 67, 127, 128, 129
cheese balls, 136
Chiswick Press, 125
Cobden-Sanderson, TJ, 105, 117, 127, 129
Cockerell, Sidney, 10, 13, 90, 128, 129
cod, Soho, 146
Comely, Philip, 79, 89, 90
Commonweal, 119, 122
Cornforth, Fanny, 67
Coronio, Aglaia, *70*, 72, 81, 83, 84
Cottier, 100
Cowper-Temple, William, 63
Crane, Walter, 11, *120*
currants: vanilla custard tart with fresh currants, 154, *155*

De Morgan, Mary, 10
De Morgan, William, 101, 104, 109, 112, 113, 116
The Defence of Guinevere, 37, 52
Democratic Federation, 116, *116*, 117
Deverell, Walter, 32
devilled herb butter, fried steaks with, 142
Dixon, Richard Watson, 23, 26, 30
Dolmetsch, Arnold, 129
Doves Bindery, 127
A Dream of John Ball, 119
duck, roast with root vegetables, 145

The Earthly Paradise, 16, 46, 64, 65-7, 70, 72, 80, 100
Eastern Question Association, 104
eggs in snow, 156
elderberry syrup, 154
Ellis, Frederick Startridge, 11, 64, 84, 91, 125, 127-8
Elm House, Walthamstow, *18*, 20
Epping Forest, 20-1
Evans, WH, 80
Exeter College, Oxford, 23, 28, 116

Fabian Society, 117-18
Faulkner, Charles, 23, 38, 46-7, 56, 80, 117, 124, 133
Faulkner, Kate, 64
The Firm, 44, 52-3, 62-3, 85, 91, 93, *94*, 132

fruit cake, rich light, 152
Fulford, William, 23, 29-30

Gere, Charles March, *123*
Giles, Mr and Mrs, 90
Gilmore, Isabella, 11
Gladstone, William, 104
Glasier, Bruce, 119-20, 132, 133
Gosse, Edmund, 65, 72
Graham, Robert Cunninghame, 11
The Grange, Fulham, *89*
Grosvenor, Hon. Richard, 112, 133
Guy, Rev. Frederick, 23, 84

halibut steaks, grilled, 146, *147*
ham and lentil soup, 134
Hammersmith Socialist Society, 11, 119, *119*, 122
Heeley, Wilfred, 30-1, 64
Horrington House, Turnham Green, 94
House of the Wolfings, 125
Howard, George, 94, 121
Howard, Rosalind, 94, 121
Howell, Mr and Mrs Charles Augustus, 64
Hughes, Arthur, 11, 33, 34, 53
Hunt, Violet, 121
Hyndman, Henry Mayers, 11, 116

Independent Labour Party, 122
International Exhibition (1862), 53
Irish stew, 140, *141*

James, Henry, 68

Kelmscott House, Hammersmith, *99*, 100, 101, *102-3*, 104-9, *107, 108*, 121-2, *126*
Kelmscott Manor, 13, 72, *74-7, 76-9, 80-2, 86-8*, 89-91, *92, 95, 96, 123*
Kelmscott Press, 16, *123*, 125-7, *127*, 128

Labour movement, 117
lamb: Irish stew, 140, *141*
  lamb in claret, *144*, 145
Lethaby, WR, 11
The Life and Death of Jason, 67
Linnell, Alfred, 119
Lushington, Vernon, 32

MacCarthy, Fiona, 26
Macdonald, George, 100

Mackail, JW, 15, 16, 51, 59, 72, 117, 122, 132
Maclaren, Archibald, 27
Macleod, Elizabeth, 112
Madox Brown, Emma, 51
Madox Brown, Ford, *16*, 33, 38, 49, 85
Magnusson, Eirikr, 80, 133
Malory, Sir Thomas, 30, 33, 34
Manning, Henry, 27
Marlborough College, 22, 23
Marshall, Peter Paul, 52-3
Marx, Eleanor, 118
Marx, Karl, 116-17
Merton Abbey, 109-10, 122
Millais, John Everett, 31
Morris, Colonel Arthur (WM's brother), 11
Morris, Edgar (WM's brother), 11, 110
Morris, Elizabeth (WM's mother), 20, 48, 49, 53, 63-4, 120
Morris, Emma (WM's sister), 20
Morris, Henrietta (WM's sister), 11, 29
Morris, Janey (WM's wife), 10, *11*, 36-8, *39*, 42, 46, 49, *52*, 56, 59, 62, 65, *65*, *66*, 67-72, 76-80, *78*, 83-5, *84*, 94, 98-9, 105, 109, 112-13, 117, 120, 124, 128
Morris, Jenny (WM's daughter), 11, *48*, 51, 76-9, *79*, 93-4, 117, 124
Morris, May (WM's daughter), 10, *48*, 52, 62, 63, 64-5, 76-9, *79*, 105, 107, 117, 120, *121*, 124, *126*
Morris, Stanley (WM's brother), 11
Morris, William (WM's father), 20, 22
Morris & Co., 91-3, 104, 109-10, 124-5
Morris, Marshall, Faulkner & Co., 52-6, 62-3, 85, *85*
mulberries, poached pears with, 152, *153*
Murray, Charles Fairfax, *15*, 76, *129*

Newman, John Henry, 27
News from Nowhere, 118, 119, 122, *123*

Orrinsmith, Mrs, 93
The Oxford and Cambridge Magazine, 31
Oxford Union, 34, *35*, 36
Oxford University, 23-6, 28, 100, 116
oysters, fried with bacon, *138*, 139

Parsons, John, *65*, 67
pears, poached with brambles or mulberries, 152, *153*

pea, lettuce and mint soup, 134, *135*
Pevsner, Nikolaus, 42
pie, veal and ham, 142, *143*
pigeons, spatchcocked with mustard sauce, 136, *137*
pike, baked with forcemeat stuffing, 148
Pine, Mrs, 127
Pollen, John Hungerford, 34
potatoes, Irish stew, 140, *141*
Powell, Messrs, 64
Pre-Raphaelite Brotherhood, 30, 31, 32
Price, Cormell (Crom), 11, 23, 26, 31, 101, 112
Prinsep, Val, 34, 37
Pusey, Professor, 27

Quaritch, Bernard, 126-7
Queen Square, London, *60*, 62, 63, 64, 68, 72, 94

rabbit, stew with apple and prunes, 146
recipes, 134-56
The Red House, Kent, *17*, *40-1*, 42-51, 53, 56-9, *56-7*
Red Lion Square, London, 32, *33*, 52
The Retreat, Hammersmith, 94, 98-100; see also Kelmscott House
Reynolds, Elizabeth, 51
The Roots of the Mountains, 125
Rossetti, Christina, 112
Rossetti, Dante Gabriel, *12*, 13-15, *14*, 29, 31-4, *35*, 36-8, 45-6, *47*, 51-2, 65, *66*, 67-8, *69*, 70-1, *70*, 72, 76-9, *78-9*, 83-9, *84*, *88*, *93*, 94, 98, 105
Ruskin, John, *12*, 27, 28, 30, 32, 51, 101

St James's Palace, 63, 116
salad, spring vegetable, *150*, 151
salted and spiced cold beef roast, 140
Scott, Sir Gilbert, 101
Scott, Sir Walter, 20, 22
Scott, William Bell, 71
Scott, Mrs William Bell, 49
seed cake, 156, *157*
The Set, 26, 27, 30
Shaw, Bernard, 49, 69, 90, 119, 120, 124, *126*, 132
Siddal, Elizabeth "Lizzie", 37, 45, 49, 51-2, 71, 105
Sigurd the Volsung, 100
Smith, Robert and Frank, 124-5
Social Democratic Federation, 117, 118

Socialist League, 118, 119-20, 122
Society for the Protection of Ancient Buildings (SPAB), 101-4
Soho cod, 146
soups, 134
South Kensington Museum, 63
Sparling, Henry Halliday, 11, 124, *126*
Spencer-Stanhope, JR, 34
spring vegetable salad, *150*, 151
Stillman, William, 71
strawberries à la Morris, 154, *155*
Street, George Edmund, 31-2
The Sundering Flood, 129
Swinburne, Algernon Charles, 51, 118

tart, vanilla custard, with fresh currants, 154, *155*
Taylor, George Warington, 62, 80, 85, 132
Tennyson, Alfred Lord, 30, 32, 56, 100, 117
Thackeray, William Makepeace, 31
Tractarian Movement, 27
trout, fried with almonds and field mushrooms, 148, *149*
Turner, Elizabeth, 76

Van Eyck, Jan, 16, *17*, 29
vanilla custard tart with fresh currants, 154, *155*
veal and ham pie, 142, *143*
Victoria, Queen, 116
Victoria and Albert Museum, 105

Walker, Emery, 11, 91, 107, 125, *126*, 127
Wardle, George, 65
Wardle, Thomas, 93
Water House, Walthamstow, *22*, 23
Watkinson, Raymond, 46
Watts, GF, 34
Webb, Philip, 13, *15*, 31, 32, *36*, 38, 42, 44-6, 49-51, 56-9, 64, 85, *86-7*, *92*, *99*, 100, 104, 117
Whistler, JMW, 49
Whitefriars Glassworks, 64
Wilberforce, Henry, 27
Wilkes, James, 119
Windus, Benjamin, 31
The Wood beyond the World, 129
Woodford Hall, Essex, 20, *21*, 132-3
Woodward, Benjamin, 34, *35*
Wren, Sir Christopher, 101

Zambaco, Marie, 72, 94